P9-DWI-000

RONALD REAGAN

Portrait of an American Hero

✦1911–2004✦

by

Tamra B. Orr

FOREWORD AND CONSULTING BY

Peter Hannaford

FORMER AIDE TO RONALD REAGAN

Publications International, Ltd.

Tamra B. Orr is the author of more than 30 nonfiction books, including *Ronald Reagan* (Childhoods of the Presidents), *The Biography of Alan Shepard Junior,* and *The Biography of Sally Ride.* A professional journalist and former newspaper columnist, she has also contributed to more than 50 national magazines.

Peter Hannaford was closely associated with Ronald Reagan for many years. During Reagan's governorship of California, Hannaford served as assistant to the governor and Reagan's director of public affairs. He went on to assume senior positions in the 1976 and 1980 Reagan presidential campaigns. In the Reagan White House years, Hannaford served on the public relations advisory committee of the United States Information Agency and was a consultant to the President's Task Force on Privatization. He is the author of many articles and nine books, including five about President Reagan: *The Reagans: A Political Portrait, Remembering Reagan* (co-author), *Recollections of Reagan, The Quotable Ronald Reagan,* and *Ronald Reagan and His Ranch: The Western White House, 1981–89.*

Acknowledgments:
The following personal writings are reprinted by permission and courtesy of President and Mrs. Ronald Reagan:

Page 75: Letter, "Dear First Lady," as it appeared in *I Love You, Ronnie: The Letters of Ronald Reagan to Nancy Reagan,* by Nancy Reagan and Ronald Reagan, © Random House, 2000.

Page 86: Letter from Ronald Reagan to the people of the United States dated November 5, 1994, in which he announced he had Alzheimer's disease.

Photo credits:

Front cover: ©**Corbis.**

Back cover: ©**Corbis:** Bettmann (top right & bottom right); Douglas Kirkland (left).

AP Wide World Photos, Inc.: Contents (bottom right), 7 (bottom), 9 (bottom), 13, 17, 24, 25, 26, 46 (bottom), 48, 50, 51, 52, 64, 65 (top), 67 (top), 68, 74, 79, 80 (top), 81 (bottom), 83 (top), 86, 88, 91 (top), 93 (top), 95 (bottom); **Brown Brothers:** 6 (bottom); ©**Corbis:** 8, 11, 19, 20, 27, 29 (bottom), 30 (top), 32 (top), 61 (bottom), 62, 71, 72, 73 (top), 77, 82, 84, 87, 90, 96; Bettmann: Title page, contents (right center), 9 (top), 14, 16, 34 (bottom), 35 (bottom), 44, 45, 46 (top), 54, 55, 56 (bottom), 57, 58, 61 (top), 69, 76; Susan Biddle/Pool/Reuters: 90 (bottom); Kevork Djansezian/Pool/Reuters: 93 (bottom); Tim Graham: 73 (bottom); Wally McNamee: 65 (bottom), 78; Michael Mulvey/Dallas Morning News: 90 (top), 91 (bottom); Jason Reed/Reuters: 92, 95 (top); Reuters NewMedia Inc.: 53; Don Rypka: 66; Schenectady Museum/Hall of Electrical History Foundation: 43; John Springer Collection: 35 (top); Ted Streshinsky: 49; Underwood & Underwood: contents (top right), 12 (top); **Eureka College Archives:** 15, 22; **Globe Photos, Inc.:** Contents (bottom left), 28, 70 (top); Alpha: 83 (bottom); Dave Chancellor/Alpha: 81 (top); Ron Mesaros: 80 (bottom); Tom Rodriguez: 85; **Peter Hannaford:** 5; **Michael Patrick/FOLIO, Inc.:** 63; **Photofest:** Contents (left center), 17, 18 (top), 30 (bottom), 31, 33, 34 (top), 37, 39, 41, 47, 70 (bottom); Courtesy Ronald Reagan Library: Contents (top left), 6 (top), 7 (top), 56 (top); United Artists: 38; Universal: 32 (bottom), 42; UPI/Bettmann: 67 (bottom); Vitagraph Inc.: 18 (bottom); Warner Bros.: 29 (top); **Courtesy Ronald Reagan Library:** 10, 12 (bottom), 60; **Roger Sandler/Peter Hannaford:** 4.

Louis Weber, CEO
Publications International, Ltd.
7373 North Cicero Avenue
Lincolnwood, Illinois 60712

Manufactured in China.

8 7 6 5 4 3 2 1

ISBN: 0-7853-9734-5

CONTENTS

FOREWORD

by Peter Hannaford

As a politician and an officeholder, Ronald Reagan often surprised, amazed, and bewildered his opponents as well as the news media and other observers. Experience taught these people little, for as the years went on he was underestimated time after time.

In 1966, when Reagan challenged the incumbent two-term governor of California, Edmund G. "Pat" Brown, Brown was convinced Reagan would be a weak opponent. In November of that year, Reagan won by a margin of nearly one million votes.

Of seven or eight Republican aspirants for the 1980 nomination, President Jimmy Carter hoped Reagan would be his opponent, for, like Brown in 1966, he believed Reagan would be easy to beat. Like many previous opponents, Carter seriously underestimated Reagan's appeal to American voters. That November, Reagan won in another landslide.

Ronal Reagan and Peter Hannaford pore over a manuscript.

The following year, the head of the air traffic controllers' union called an illegal strike. Reagan announced that any striker who did not report to work within 48 hours would be fired. The union official thought he was bluffing. Reagan did just what he said he would do. That was the end of the union. And, with some effort, the planes continued to fly.

Why was Reagan frequently underestimated? There is no single explanation, but one was a widespread belief that an actor is not to be taken seriously. What was often overlooked, however, was the effectiveness with which Reagan led the Screen Actors Guild as he dealt with unions and management during labor negotiations.

As Reagan's political star rose nationally, he encountered a certain bias among the nation's "opinion elite." This collection of media people, academics, policy advisers, and financial market pundits centered on an axis running from Boston to New York to Washington. They took it for granted that anything that happened outside that East Coast axis was of secondary importance. Geography reinforced this view. California, being far away and more-or-less self-contained, was seen not for what it was—a strong, prosperous state—but rather as a land of misfits and eccentrics.

At a 1980 campaign news conference, a reporter asked Reagan what qualification he had for becoming President of the United States. Reagan told him he had governed the largest U.S. public body second to the federal government. Moreover, he developed a clear philosophy of government and found steady reinforcement for his views during his years in office. He was secure in his values, and he was not plagued with constant self-doubt.

Opponents, many media figures, and other observers could not bring themselves to take him at face value—to believe that he meant what he said. They would attribute his successes to his being "The Great Communicator." It is true he had a gift for communication and had honed that gift over a long period of time. Yet, good communication skills are of little more than entertainment value if the speaker does not have a message that connects with the concerns of the audience. Reagan learned this when he gave his first major address, and the lesson never left him.

In his freshman year (1928) at Eureka College in Illinois when the college proposed severe faculty and program cutbacks in the face of economic difficulties, a group of students organized a strike. When they looked for the "right" person to propose it at a student assembly, the leaders chose "Dutch" Reagan. His passionate speech roused the students to action, which prevented many of the proposed cutbacks and led to the resignation of the college president. Reagan had experienced what he called the "heady wine" of connecting emotionally with an audience over a shared value.

Peter Hannaford

This extraordinary book will take you through the many periods of Ronald Reagan's life. You will see how his mother's strong faith and his father's love of a good story helped shape his outlook and personality; how he went from radio to a career as a movie star, to television, to leading a union, to politics, to the governorship of California, and, finally, to become the 40th President of the United States. It is an only-in-America story.

CHAPTER ONE

"FAT LITTLE DUTCHMAN"

From humble beginnings, Reagan would learn faith, tolerance, and optimism—lessons that lasted a lifetime.

Ronald Reagan was one of those presidents who a great many people recall with a special smile or a memory, even if they didn't necessarily agree with his politics. While some may have laughed at the idea that a former movie actor could ever become president, it was actually the very skills that he had learned on the screen that helped him become such a popular leader. He was comfortable talking with people, had no problem memorizing his speeches, had a ready sense of humor, and was familiar with cameras and being in the spotlight.

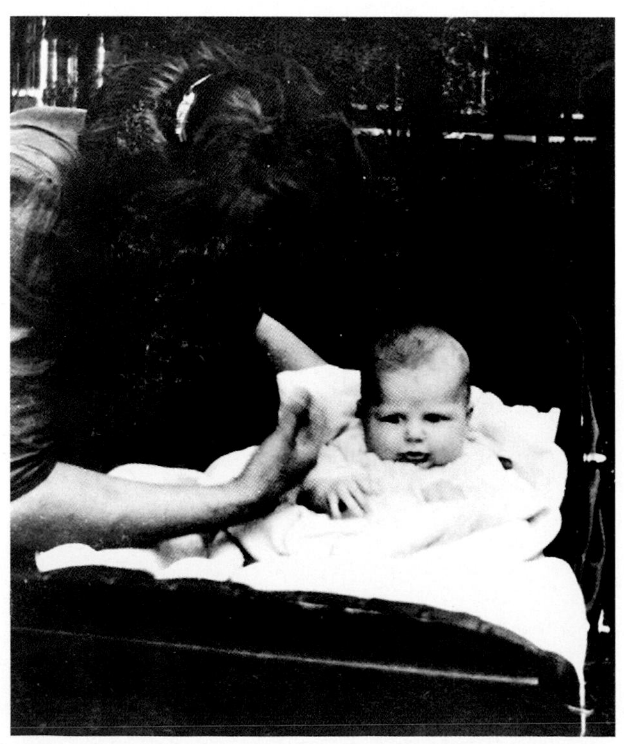

Baby Reagan in his stroller.

Reagan's sense of humor worked well with the media, and it was obvious that his love for this nation was founded on patriotism and a belief in America's foundations. It is little surprise that Reagan became known as the "Great Communicator" because he had a knack for clearly explaining things to people. Even when his decisions as president did not go as he or the nation wanted them to, his popularity held strong. He was even referred to as the "Teflon President" because nothing negative or unpleasant seemed to stick to him for long.

Reagan's many accomplishments are even more impressive when details about his early life come to light. He survived many things that could have been obstacles, including frequent moves as a small child, chronic poverty, and an alcoholic father. Despite these disadvantages, Reagan grew up with important values such as a solid work ethic, a strong faith, and a firm belief in the equality of all people—thanks to valuable lessons learned from his mother, Nelle, and his father, Jack.

Nelle Clyde Wilson, whose ancestors hailed from Scotland and England, was a small woman in stature but certainly not in personality. With her auburn hair and sparkling blue eyes, Nelle was a devout woman who deeply believed that everything in life happens according to God's plan. When she met John Edward "Jack" Reagan in the J. W. Broadhead Dry Goods Store, where they both worked in Fulton, Illinois, she was sure

Dutch is nine months old and already has that charming smile he would express on the silver screen and while in office. A somber three-year-old Neil looks on.

it was the Lord's design that she fall completely in love with this tall, charming, handsome man.

Jack had already had a tough life by the time he met his future wife. Both of his parents had died in 1889 from tuberculosis. He had been a child of six at the time. For the next six years, he was passed from one relative's home to another. At 12, he left school and started working. Despite his limited formal education, Jack was a bright man. An Irish Catholic, he hated bigotry and racism. These were lessons he would share with his sons as they grew up. Jack had a flair for the dramatic and often would dazzle people with his stories. One who was quickly swept away by his charisma was Nelle. They married in November 1904.

During the early years of their marriage, they learned more about each other and their inherent differences. While Nelle was a perennial optimist, always finding the bright side of even the most dismal of situations, Jack was quietly unhappy. Determined to be a successful salesman, he moved restlessly from place to place and job to job in search of that elusive success. It was a pattern he would follow for much of his life.

Nelle stood by him during each move, focusing her attention on her two young sons. John Neil was born on September 16, 1908, and Jack soon nicknamed him "Moon" after a popular comic strip character of the time, Moon Mullins. On February 6, 1911, a hefty ten-pound brother named Ronald Wilson was born in the middle of a winter blizzard. When Jack first saw him and heard his cry, he said he looked like "a fat little Dutchman." The nickname "Dutch" would stay with Reagan for many years. According to his own writings as a youth, he preferred the nickname since it sounded far more rugged than "Ronald." The two boys, on the other hand, would always refer to their parents, not as "Mother and Father" or "Mom and Dad," but by their first names, an indication of their respect for and equality with their parents.

When their second son was born, the Reagans were living in a small, five-room apartment above a bakery in Tampico, Illinois, and were struggling financially. The home had no indoor toilet, central heat, or running water; however, they didn't stay there for long. Between 1914 and 1920, the Reagan family moved from one Illinois town to another, including Chicago, Galesburg, Monmouth, and back to Tampico. At each place, Jack was sure he would find a job as

As a child, young Reagan moved quite often, but no matter where he was, he enjoyed spending time outdoors, observing nature and appreciating the beauty he found there. His mother taught him to love nature, and her lessons stayed with him throughout his life.

a shoe salesman and make it big. He even went so far as to take a correspondence course to learn about the individual bones of the feet in the hope of finding success. Each time, however, he was wrong and the family barely made it from paycheck to paycheck.

Jack was already finding solace in alcohol. Nelle felt it was imperative to keep her family together. While she certainly knew about Jack's drinking, she chose to see it as a disease and not as a character flaw; she encouraged her boys to perceive it the same way. No matter what town she lived in, she attended church several times a week, and her faith remained strong and an inspiration to her youngest son.

Nelle also enjoyed her time in the spotlight and would do dramatic readings at her church, organizing religious plays that she herself had written. Many times she would recruit young Ronald to be part of the act. She went to the local jail to read to prisoners and to hospitals to see the patients. Moreover, her dedication to the church and the comfort she found in it made a lasting impression on her sons.

One of the first houses the Reagans lived in was located near railroad tracks. One day, Nelle looked out to see 18-month-old Ronald and his four-year-old brother Neil crawling under a stopped train. There was an ice wagon on the other side. Just then, the whistle blew, signaling

THE DISASTER OF 1918

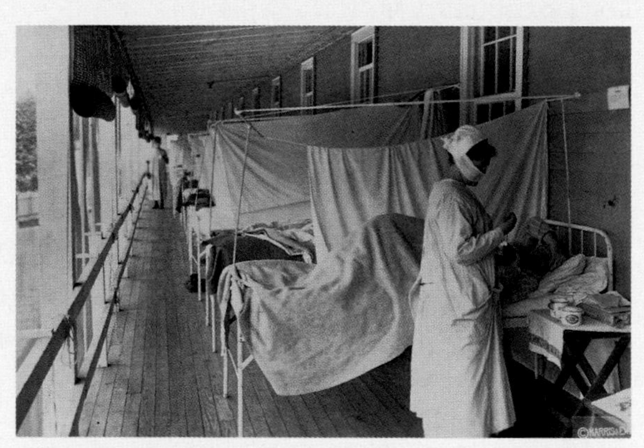

An influenza ward at Walter Reed Hospital during the plague of 1918.

In 1918, almost all of the newspaper headlines were focused on World War I—the latest news of battles, victories, and losses. It didn't seem as though any news story could possibly come along and knock the war into second place. Alas, however, one of the worst infectious outbreaks to ever hit the planet occurred the year the war ended.

The flu pandemic that year was terrifying for people the world over. Not a single country escaped it. In the end, the virus killed approximately 675,000 Americans and more than 25 million people around the globe. Even President Woodrow Wilson suffered a bout of it when he was in France to negotiate the Versailles Peace Treaty.

Victims died quickly, often from fluid in their lungs. Secondary infections set in rapidly, and since antibiotics didn't exist yet, there was little treatment at all. Without any real protection against this mysterious and determined flu, everyone was vulnerable. Recent studies from the Armed Forces Institute of Pathology suggest that the virus most resembled the kind that infect swine, and some now suspect that it attacked humans after going through pigs.

It was one of the world's darkest times as physicians and researchers fought to find the cause and the cure, to little avail. The flu arrived in Illinois when Reagan was in third grade. Schools were closed, and people went about wearing face masks in the hope of filtering out the lethal germs. Nelle was one of those who came down with the illness. For weeks, quiet and gloom resided in the Reagan household. Finally, much to the family's relief, Nelle, unlike most, was lucky—and survived.

The Reagan family in southern Chicago in 1913. Jack and Nelle stand proudly on either side of their sons Neil to the left at age four and Dutch to the right at age two.

the train was about to pull out of the station. Nelle almost stopped breathing, but before she could react, both boys safely reached the other side and made their way over to the ice. She caught up with her wandering sons just as they were reaching for some ice from the ice wagon.

Young Reagan was a quiet child, spending much of his time alone in the middle of one daydream or another. It was hard to make new friends when you were always the new kid in a school. While his family lived in Galesburg, young Reagan discovered two fascinating things in life. The first was the wonder and appreciation of the natural world, thanks to a collection of bird eggs and butterflies left in glass cases in the attic of the rented house. He spent hours looking at them, and soon was spending time outdoors exploring nearby streams, forests, and fields. Second, at the age of five, Reagan taught himself to read. His parents didn't quite believe him when he declared that he was reading the newspaper to himself, but he proved it when he read aloud from it. Jack flew out the front door and brought all the neighbors over to listen to him read aloud. Soon he was devouring adventure books, including his favorites about Tom Swift and Edgar Rice Burroughs's Martian series. He also loved westerns, little knowing that one day he would be starring in the same kind of stories that had fascinated him.

Another area that interested young Reagan was sports. In the summer of 1920, he played his first football game and was hooked. Football would continue as a passion for the rest of his life, along with swimming and track. Other games—such as tennis—simply confused him.

Baseball was frightening for him because it seemed as if the ball materialized out of thin air when it was only inches from his head, and all he could do was duck. What he didn't realize for several years was that the ball seemed to appear so suddenly because he couldn't see it until it got that close. It wasn't until Reagan was 13 years old and playfully tried on his mother's eyeglasses that he realized he hadn't been seeing things as clearly as other people did. In his mind, everyone saw things best close-up—it was normal for things to be blurry from a few feet away. Nelle took him to the optometrist, and he was fitted with thick, black-framed glasses. Now he could see, but he hated the glasses, and virtually no early pictures exist that show him wearing them. Later, Reagan would be one of the first people to

Although Reagan lived in a number of different houses in Illinois, this one in Dixon is the one that he remembered best and has been named his official boyhood home. When he toured it as an adult in 1990, he also stopped to visit with the Dixon High School football team.

Young Reagan is standing reflectively first left in the second row with his third grade classmates.

wear the new invention for poor eyesight—contact lenses.

In December 1920, a new opportunity came along that brought the family hope once more. Jack was offered a chance to be a partner in a Fashion Boot shop in Dixon, Illinois, a farming town with a population of about eight thousand, one hundred miles west of Chicago. Although the family lived in five different homes in Dixon and the boot shop turned out to be another failure, they stayed there for 12 years. Reagan always considered Dixon his hometown. In his future writings and speeches, he would refer to the city in glowing terms, frequently comparing his childhood there to a Tom Sawyer–Huck Finn existence.

Despite Reagan's sunny portrayal of his years in Dixon, they were not easy ones. Jack's drinking escalated, and occasionally he would be gone for days on a binge. The Reagan's marriage was under constant stress, not only because of the drinking but also because of their religious differences. Jack was a Catholic while Nelle was a Protestant, and neither would convert to the other's belief. Despite it all, Nelle kept the marriage together, even when there wasn't enough money to put food on the table or Jack had been gone for several days. It was obvious that the two of them loved each other, but physical affection was limited.

For the most part, Reagan did his best to ignore what was happening with his father. One day, however, something occurred that made it impossible for him to overlook it anymore. At the age of 11, he came home from a YMCA basketball game to find his father passed out on the front lawn during a snowstorm. It was a critical moment for him. Should he walk on by and pretend he hadn't seen his father? Or, should he pull him into the house even if that felt humiliating? Finally, in spite of his embarrassment, Reagan dragged his father inside the house and tucked him into bed. In later years, he would refer to this moment as the one where he truly felt that he had begun to mature and take responsibility for his actions.

Reagan attended the Disciples of Christ Church with his mother and soon taught some of the Sunday school classes himself. The faith he learned there, as well as that modeled by Nelle, became an integral part of his values. It would remain so throughout his life, through the temptations of Hollywood and through the stresses and dilemmas in the world of politics.

Although Jack was often a distant, drunken, and frustrated father, he, too, managed to impart some valuable principles to his sons. The primary one was tolerance and fairness to people of all classes and races. The early 20th century was still a time of deep racism in parts of America, with segregated schools and other public places. This angered Jack, which he expressed to his sons, who, for example, were forbidden to see the new movie *Birth of a Nation*, which was sweeping the country. Jack felt that the film promoted racial prejudice by including positive scenes about the Ku Klux Klan. Another example came with a hefty price tag for him. When Jack was on the road and went to check into a hotel and discovered that Jews were not allowed, he walked back out to his car and spent the night in it, getting pneumonia in the process. Nevertheless, it taught his boys an important lesson. When Ronald Reagan was in high school and college and played on teams that included African American teammates, he always knew that he could bring them to his house to spend the night if an area hotel wouldn't accept them. In his home, all people were equal and welcomed. Neil's best friend was African American, and when they went to the movies, Neil sat right there in the balcony with his friend.

Jack also taught some lessons in discipline to his sons. One time he bought a carload of second-hand potatoes and assigned them the unpleasant job of sorting the good from the bad. Even as an adult, Reagan would recall this experience with a shudder, remembering the feel of a rotten potato dissolving between his fingers and the bad smell that came from it. The two boys separated potatoes for several days. In the end, they dumped the whole batch because they couldn't stand looking at one more rotten spud.

As Reagan approached his teen years, he was still a rather short, thin boy hampered by his thick, black eyeglasses. In the next few years, however, that boy would quickly disappear, and a tall, charismatic, and talented young man would emerge—just in time for high school and girls.

At age 12, Reagan poses in Dixon, Illinois. It was the town he would think of as home. It was the kind of close, gentle, and loyal place that he wished most of the nation could be.

CHAPTER TWO

A GRAND, SWEET SONG

From sunny summer days at Rock River to young love, Reagan grows into a strong young man.

The teenage Ronald Reagan bore little resemblance to the small boy in elementary school pictures, although the changes came more slowly than he wanted them to. When he entered high school, he still stood about 5′3″ and weighed a mere 108 pounds. After years of staring at the mannequins in white-and-purple high school football uniforms in a downtown store in Dixon, Reagan was determined to play football. The first year he tried out, the coach struggled just to find a uniform to fit him, and he didn't make the team. Reagan was greatly disappointed. Time, however, would change this picture.

Not surprisingly, the job at the Fashion Boot store had not worked out for Jack. Once again, he was out hunting for a job as his family packed up their belongings in an all-too-familiar process and moved to a smaller, less expensive house in Dixon. Their new location meant the boys could choose which high school they wanted to attend, and in a typical example of the personality differences between Reagan and his brother, Neil, they chose different schools. Ronald tended to model after his mother and to follow her interests, while Neil followed in his father's footsteps, loving a good story peppered with Irish charm.

Neil chose one high school because of its sports program, while Ronald went to a different high school because of its concentration on the arts. Ronald was relieved because he frequently

Neil Reagan is second from the left in the front row.

felt as if he lived in his big brother's shadow. This way, there wouldn't be as much of a comparison between the two brothers. In later years, they would become much closer, but for now, they were rivals.

Like many teenagers today, Reagan's summers were filled with a variety of temporary jobs. In 1925, both he and Neil worked as roustabouts for the Ringling Brothers Circus when it came to town, making about a quarter an hour. They would work in the predawn darkness, dragging circus wagons into the mud so they wouldn't roll away and bringing food to the animals' cages. Reagan also caddied at the local golf course and spent many hours working on construction jobs. There he learned how to lay hardwood floors, shingle roofs, and paint ceilings. He even dug foundations for 35 cents an hour.

One very hot morning on the job, Reagan had a dangerously close call with his boss. After four hours of swinging a heavy pick, he was so relieved to hear the noon whistle blow that he swung his pick to the ground. It landed right between his boss's feet! It was questionable who had the bigger scare. The hard work Reagan did all summer with his pick and shovel built up the muscles he needed for the football field, but it did not help his short height.

Fortunately, when he returned to Dixon High, the high school football conference had developed a new division for smaller players up to 135 pounds. Not only did Reagan make that team, he was elected captain of it, and he played both tackle and guard. By the following year, nature had sped up the growth process, and Reagan was no longer a scrawny kid. Instead, he stood almost 6 feet in height and weighed 160 pounds. By mid-season of his junior year, he was on the varsity team and its first-string squad. In his senior year, Reagan also played on the school's basketball and track teams, doing well at both sports.

During Reagan's second year in high school, he stumbled across what would be one of his all-time favorite jobs—lifeguarding. When the Dixon Park Commission was considering closing the local Lowell Park because of several drownings that had occurred there, Reagan spoke up and asked them to allow him to be the park's lifeguard. He had taken lifeguard courses at the local

Football was a passion of young Reagan from an early age, but it took a long time for his size to catch up to his ambitions. Meanwhile, he was on the lightweight team, which played before the varsity for all of the regular season games. Here he is, seated second from right in the front row.

Reagan's job as lifeguard at Lowell Park always brought a smile to his face. It was here that he developed muscles and confidence to join his college football team.

YMCA, and he was an excellent swimmer—just what the job required.

The park commission agreed to give him a try. For seven summers—throughout high school and into his college years—Reagan was lifeguard at Lowell Park, a 300-acre forested recreational park bordering the Rock River. It had been named after the local poet James Russell Lowell. Sitting high up on his special chair on the beach, Reagan remembers getting his first taste of being in the limelight, and he liked it. He worked long days, often putting in 12 hours—10 A.M. to 10 P.M.—seven days a week for a take-home check of $15 a week and all the hamburgers and root beer he wanted. To earn a few more dollars, he also taught swimming to the kids who could afford it.

Reagan enjoyed every minute of his lifeguard job, and he made a significant difference in his community. During the course of his seven years there, he rescued 77 lives and was featured in the local newspaper time and again. He kept track of his rescues on a nearby log, making a new notch for each person brought back to shore safely.

In addition to keeping an eye on swimmers, Reagan was expected to pick up food supplies for the park. This involved getting a 300-pound block of ice and breaking it into three 100-pound pieces to put in coolers. On extra hot days, it might mean more than one trip to get that huge block of ice. He ate his meals on duty, and when the day was about over, he helped clean up the beach. Thanks to all his lifting and swimming, Reagan was building strong muscles and a physique that was definitely getting the attention of many of the young ladies at the beach.

Reagan loved this new attention, but one day he saw a face that made all of the others just fade away. The face belonged to a girl named Margaret Cleaver, and she would turn out to be his first real love. Summers were now spent working and having dates with his steady girl "Mugs," as he called her.

Along with his summer jobs, Reagan excelled in different areas at school. His abilities as a leader were already apparent, and he was becoming a person whom teachers, staff,

MARGARET "MUGS" CLEAVER

Long before Jane Wyman and Nancy Davis came along, Reagan's greatest love was a young woman named Margaret Cleaver. Although most of her friends and family called her Peggy, "Mugs" was the special nickname Reagan had for her. They first met in high school and dated each other exclusively in their senior year. The two remained sweethearts during their college years at Eureka. Daughter of a Christian Church minister, the Reverend Ben Cleaver, Mugs was usually at the top of her class. In her high school yearbook, she was described as "our popular all-around everything." Short and pretty, Mugs had dark eyes and dark hair as well as a sparkling sense of humor.

College photo of Margaret Cleaver

The Cleavers were progressive thinkers, firmly believing in the rights and equality of women. Mugs, along with her two sisters, were encouraged to pursue their educational interests as well as do some world traveling. Because of his affection for their daughter, Reagan was a welcome addition to their family gatherings; Reverend Cleaver was something of a father figure for Reagan at the time.

Summers were spent on canoe dates at Lowell Park, where Reagan would row the boat onto the water and play music on an old wind-up Victrola as they munched on a picnic meal. Other dates were spent skating at the roller rink, getting two-cent cherry phosphates at the local drugstore counter, or going to the movies. Many a romantic moment was spent in an old graveyard close to where they attended college.

All their friends assumed Mugs and Dutch would marry one day—and so did Reagan. After graduation from college, however, Mugs took a trip to Europe and upon her return, she sent him a letter telling him that she planned to marry another man, James Waddell Gordon, Jr., whom she had met on the trip. Their breakup was hard on Reagan, but he bought a new brown two-seater Nash La Fayette convertible to cheer himself up, and before long, he was back out on the dating circuit.

and students all noticed and remembered. Meanwhile, his character, presence, and comfort in the limelight were growing. While he wasn't the best academic student, usually making B's and C's in his classes, Reagan knew how to organize people and lead them. These were skills he would one day use on a routine basis.

During his four years at Dixon High, Reagan was not only elected president of the Dixon Student Council but also the president of his senior class. As vice president of the Hi-Y Club, a local youth group, he helped uphold its motto of "Clean Sports, Clean Living, and Clean Scholarship." In addition to these accomplishments, he was a drum major in the school band. In his senior year at Dixon High, Reagan served as the art director of his class yearbook. Interestingly, he designed it around the theme of a movie or theater set, with students billed as cast, directors, producers, and scriptwriters. Little did he know how much a part of his world all those different roles would one day become!

One of the faculty members who noticed Reagan's growing talents was an English and history teacher, B. J. Fraser. It was Fraser who introduced the idea of serious acting to Reagan—a step that would lead him to fame and fortune in the years to come. Fraser encouraged Reagan to write essays and read them aloud to the class. Reagan enjoyed making his classmates laugh, and he wrote humorous essays to entertain his peers. He also wrote poetry and short stories.

Fraser urged Reagan to audition for school plays, and it wasn't long before both teacher and student recognized a great match. Reagan was a natural actor with an excellent memory, which made remembering lines an easy task. He loved being on stage and having the attention of an audience. During his years in high school, he played the role of Ricky in Philip Barry's *You and I* and the villain in George Bernard Shaw's *Captain Applejack*. He also starred with Mugs in a one-act play called *The Pipe of Peace*, and the two sweethearts would go on to perform in a number of other plays after they graduated and entered Eureka College together. Fraser was an excellent coach and director, giving Reagan his first real lessons about how to analyze a character and become that person on stage. This instruction would later serve as the foundation for the routine Reagan would use when he acted in films.

High school was a wonderful time for Reagan. He did well in everything he tried, and he was

Young Reagan poses on the far right in the back row with other members of the high school Dramatics Society and with their instructor, B. J. Fraser, seated in the front row in the center.

During his years at Dixon High School, Reagan appeared on the stage a number of times. Here he can be seen, fifth from left, in the role of Ivan Borolsky, the villain in Captain Applejack.

widely popular, due in large part to his positive and pleasant attitude. Under his yearbook photograph is a quote from one of his own poems that exemplified his outlook: "Life is just one grand, sweet song, so start the music."

Reagan's dream of playing football came true, but he also had another dream—one that seemed much less apt to become reality, considering the shaky economic times. As he prepared to graduate from high school in 1928, the country was little more than a year away from a stock market crash, to be followed in the thirties by the Great Depression.

Reagan was determined to go on to college even though less than 7 percent of the nation's high school graduates were financially able to do that. He already knew where he wanted to go: a Christian liberal arts college located about 80 miles south of Dixon. This was the school that his sweetheart, Mugs, was going to as well as the one that Reagan's long-time football hero, former Dixon high school fullback Garland Waggoner, had attended. There was no way Nelle and Jack would be able to pay for a college education for either of their sons, but that didn't slow down Reagan for a moment. He had faith that—as his mother always reassured him—the Lord would provide. Thanks to his prowess in swimming and football, that is just what happened.

Reagan's senior picture from his 1928 high school yearbook contained an error in the caption, listing him as Donald instead of Ronald.

CHAPTER THREE

THE COLLEGE YEARS AT EUREKA

A taste of power and a talent for drama set the stage for Reagan's later years.

Childhood was far behind Ronald Reagan and young adulthood was just around the corner when he entered college. Eureka was not like the other colleges of the era. These were the days of raccoon coats, bobbed hair, and Prohibition (and contraband alcohol, but not at Eureka). This was a college—in fact, an entire city—that didn't allow alcohol anywhere inside its borders. There was little to no crime for miles. Dancing on campus was forbidden, a strict dress code was enforced—with skirt lengths measured and the color of hose severely limited—and daily chapel attendance was mandatory for all 250 students.

Because of Reagan's strong church background, Eureka seemed just the right college for him. In many ways, this college exemplified the values that he held dear: racial tolerance, the Bible, and high moral standards. He had fallen in love with the rural 114-acre campus the first time he visited. He was grateful to be there since, until a matter of days before his first semester began, he didn't believe he would be able to afford it. A last-minute scholarship—arranged in part by the Reverend Cleaver and based on athletic performance, not grades—paid $180 of his tuition and $270 of his room and board. The rest of the money he had come up with himself from his job at Lowell Park.

Of course, this left nothing for spending money, so Reagan spent most of his college years supplementing his income by doing various jobs such as washing dishes in his fraternity house and several sorority houses, waiting tables,

Reagan was an avid swimmer throughout his life.

A long line at a soup kitchen during the Great Depression.

raking leaves, and even thawing out frozen water pipes in the winter. He also made extra money as the swimming coach and through one of the jobs he already knew quite well—lifeguarding—at the college pool. Reagan sent part of the money he earned home, as the Depression drew closer and his father was out of work once more.

For a while, Nelle and Jack separated, and neighbors were sure they would divorce. By this time Jack had a new job as a traveling shoe salesman, and he rented an apartment several hundred miles from Dixon. The split was temporary, however, as Nelle was determined to keep her family together. Within a matter of months, they were reunited. She began working in a dress shop for $14 a week. At college Ronald managed to send $50 a month home to help make ends meet. Jack was never told about this arrangement because it would have dealt a humiliating blow to the pride of a man who had experienced more than his share of humiliation. Experiencing the long years of poverty at home and seeing the tragic effects the Depression had on people combined to make financial security a high priority for Ronald Reagan the rest of his life.

Reagan's freshman year was a busy one—and not just academically. He took classes in rhetoric, French, history, English literature, math, and physical education. Of course, swimming and football were squeezed in as well as theater. During his years at Eureka, Reagan spent far more time in extracurricular activities than he did in class. Although he majored in economics and social science, that was not what Reagan was remembered for at Eureka. During his four years, he was made captain of the track team, coach of the swim team, president of the Booster Club, yearbook features editor, student body president, captain of the basketball cheerleaders, editor of the campus newsletter, and president of the student council. He was on the school debate team and a member of Tau Kappa Epsilon fraternity. It was little surprise that, with all of this going on, he just managed to keep a C average in most of his classes.

Reagan's biggest advantage at Eureka was the same one that had carried him through high

A photo of the Eureka College football team. Reagan is fourth from right in the front row.

school—his ability to read something once and retain it for later use. Here at Eureka he could use this skill to catch up with material quickly to pass many of his tests. This is the same skill that would one day help him learn speeches quickly and then deliver them to the American people so convincingly.

Reagan's freshman year was not only a hectic one, but it also featured an incident he would never forget. It gave him his first real taste of holding an audience in his hand, not as an actor playing a role, but as himself. The ability to excite and lead a group of people with his own words, instead of the lines from a script, so uplifted and thrilled him that he would carry the memory of this experience throughout his life. Quite likely, this was also one of those defining moments in life that help guide a person in one direction or another. For Reagan, it was one of the most important steps he would take in the direction of a political career.

In this case, the issue was not world politics but campus politics. Eureka may have been a wonderful college and just what Reagan had hoped for, but it was also in trouble. Although the Depression hadn't officially hit yet, rumblings of what was to come were in the air, and colleges were feeling the financial shortages. This was especially true at rural Eureka, where donations were a large part of the annual budget. Contributions were down; enrollment was down. Some professors were teaching classes but not receiving paychecks. Cuts were inevitable, and it fell to the shoulders of college President Bert Wilson to make the cuts. He felt drastic measures were called for to save the college, and his decisions were decidedly unpopular.

In order to keep the college going, Wilson believed several measures were needed: Departments must be consolidated; certain programs, such as art, home economics, and sports, would be dropped; and some teachers would be laid off. No one was happy with Wilson—from the students, who worried that their academic standing or graduation would be jeopardized if the classes they still needed were dropped, to the faculty, who didn't know how they would cope if they lost their jobs during hard times. To make matters worse for Wilson, he was also critical of the Eureka community itself, saying that it no longer supported the college. He spoke of moving the entire school to an area that had more churches as potential contributors. The townspeople didn't appreciate his lack of faith in them. Despite this, in mid-November of 1928, just before the school broke for the holidays, the school board accepted

Wilson's suggestions, and that is when events really heated up.

Bert Wilson was hampered by the fact that he was already not popular on the college campus, thanks to several other issues that had occurred earlier. Although dancing had been banned at Eureka for some time, some students objected. At the annual get-acquainted party held in the fall, they banded together and convinced the orchestra to play some dance music. Wilson put an immediate stop to it, making the so-called rebels come up on the stage for a public scolding. Next, Wilson pushed for tighter restrictions on students as well as harsher discipline for those who broke the rules. When the board supported Wilson's new decisions, students were incensed. They called for his resignation, and although he finally gave it, the board, after six days of deliberation, would not accept it. It was time for action on the part of the students. It would be the first student protest in the history of the college.

Although Reagan was only a freshman at the time, he had already established himself on the small campus as a man who had presence and the power to attract attention. He was elected to be the representative for the students. Late at night, before everyone could take off for Thanksgiving break, Reagan called a student meeting and proceeded to deliver a speech that he would remember for years to come. He spoke of the importance of students standing up for what they believed and speaking out, and then he urged students to strike until Wilson was overruled. After Reagan finished his speech, a vote was taken and a strike was approved. Students were on their feet cheering and yelling, and Reagan felt the thrill of knowing he had galvanized his audience to action. It was a feeling he would experience many times in his life, but few would be as exhilarating as this one.

When the holiday break was over, students returned to Eureka, but very few of them actually returned to their classes. Instead, they

BEFORE HOLLYWOOD

Long before Reagan realized he would be spending a good portion of his life on the silver screen, he spent time on the stages of schools, from Dixon High to Eureka. While he enjoyed acting, the thought of making acting a career was not yet born—and with good reason. In an era when unemployment would soon reach 26 percent, anyone saying he or she wanted to be a film star would have been ridiculed. However, when the Reverend Cleaver happened to take Reagan and Mugs to see *Journey's End* (a play about World War I) during Thanksgiving break of 1928, Reagan was so swept away that he knew acting was exactly what he wanted to do with his life.

This feeling was further vindicated in his junior year when Reagan and Mugs participated in a national competition of one-act plays at the annual Eva Le Gallienne Competition held at Northwestern University. Reagan played a Greek shepherd boy who is strangled in Edna St. Vincent Millay's antiwar play, *Aria da Capo*. Eureka College took second place at the competition, which was exciting, but then the names of the actors who had won individual acting awards were announced—and Reagan's was one of them. It was the confirmation he needed to know that acting was the right path for him.

During his college years, whenever Reagan appeared in a play, the reviews would always point out his amazing stage presence. Critics would note how he seemed to draw the attention of the audience even if his character was a secondary one.

stayed in their dorms and apartments in silent protest to Wilson's plan. Teachers, also angry over the situation, cooperated with the students by not reporting them absent. This continued until the end of the first week of December. It wasn't long before Wilson's resignation was given again. This time the board accepted it. The story made national news, with articles in *The New York Times* and the *Chicago Tribune*. Reporters combed the campus to report on this little school with big ideas. Reagan felt he had played a significant role in this initial foray into politics, and the memory of it would stay with him.

By now, Reagan had reached his full height of 6′1″ and weighed about 175 pounds. He was a force to be reckoned with on the football field, and he played first-string guard for Eureka's Golden Tornadoes for all four years. He earned four letters under the watchful eye of Coach Ralph McKinzie. His performance on the college swim team was impressive as well. During his freshman year, he won most of the individual events, such as the crawl stroke and the backstroke. The only one he didn't conquer was the breaststroke. In reality, swimming was more his athletic strength than football, but swimming did not bring him the sense of physical accomplishment he received from football.

During the summers, Reagan returned to Dixon and his old job in the lifeguard chair at Lowell Park. Dixon welcomed him home with open arms—proud of one of their own who was actually making it in college during a time when few did. He and Mugs still shared their mutual passion for theater and drama. Fortunately, the college had just hired a new drama teacher, who would help Reagan develop his growing skills. Ellen Marie Johnson took theater quite seriously, and instead of just concentrating on an annual play, she had her students performing year-round and in area competitions. Reagan and Mugs would share the stage a number of times, and their relationship continued to grow, convincing almost everyone who knew them that marriage would follow graduation. Even when Mugs decided to attend the University of Illinois in her

Eureka College in the early 1930s.

junior year, she and Reagan stayed together, despite the distance. Mugs then returned to Eureka for her senior year.

When Reagan left home for college his first year, he had packed his belongings in a shiny, new steamer trunk. It was his pride and joy. Each year, he would bring his things home in that trunk, and each fall, he would pack it once again to return. At the end of his freshman year, he went home for the summer, as usual. This time he had a surprise with him. While he had been attending college, his brother, Neil, had been working at a Dixon cement plant, choosing to work instead of attending college. Because Reagan wanted more for his big brother, he had arranged through some of his contacts not only a scholarship for Neil but also a part-time job. To his surprise, Neil turned down the offer.

Reagan and his mother were disappointed when Neil refused to go, but in a show of continual hope and optimism, Reagan made one last gesture to his brother. Packing up his own things in cardboard boxes, he headed off to Eureka for his sophomore year. When Neil came home from work that day, he saw Ronald's steamer trunk sitting in the middle of his bedroom. The statement was clear. When he talked at the cement plant the next day about what his brother had done for him, he laughed at the foolishness of it all. His boss, however, wasn't laughing, and that afternoon Neil was given his last paycheck. His boss had decided that if Neil wasn't bright enough to take an offer like the one his brother had made, he wasn't smart enough to work at the plant. Neil enrolled at Eureka the following afternoon. The bond between the two young men began to strengthen, despite their distinctly different personalities.

When Ronald Reagan graduated from Eureka in 1932, the message written underneath his yearbook picture was an accurate one: "The time never lies heavily upon him, it is impossible for him to be alone." In his own mind, he had already decided that Hollywood was the place he wanted to be, but he also realized that his dream of being a movie star was an unlikely one, especially with the country's economic stress. The Depression was in full swing, and all around him people were losing their jobs, their homes, and their futures. It was hard to face that and keep the dream of becoming an actor a realistic one.

Before Reagan tried to cross the country to a distant California—and Hollywood—he decided to start a little closer to home. Chicago wasn't far, and it held great potential for a would-be film star who was willing to first try his hand at being a radio announcer. Before he left Eureka, Reagan bet all of his fraternity brothers that within five years he would be earning $5,000 a year. No one believed him, for that was approximately $2,000 more than a physician made in the early 1930s. He hoped he was right, but at the back of his mind, he worried about what Mugs would think of his career aspirations and whether she would want to be married to an actor.

Money was a constant concern. Although his father now handled the local welfare office and had recently been hired as an investigator at the Dixon branch of the Illinois Emergency Relief Commission, Ronald knew that Nelle would still need the monthly contributions he had been sending. Before he headed off to unknown possibilities in Chicago, he decided to spend just one more season as lifeguard at Lowell Park to earn the money he would need to get started.

Decades after he left Eureka, Reagan would return to his alma mater with pride. In 1947, he was Grand Marshall of the college's fifth annual Pumpkin Parade. He rode in the parade, put the crown on the head of the newly elected Pumpkin Queen, and danced with her at the ball. Twenty years later, in 1967, as governor of California, he returned once again to be honored as Eureka's most famous graduate. In January 1976, by then a candidate for the Republican presidential nomination, he returned for a rally in the Dixon High School gymnasium and a visit to Lowell Park.

CHAPTER FOUR

LIGHTS, CAMERA, ACTION!

From on the air to on the screen, Reagan's star is on the rise—and then along comes World War II.

After that one last summer spent sitting in the lifeguard chair, Reagan was finally ready to put Dixon behind him and move forward with his more ambitious plans. He knew that radio was a good place to start because, despite the dire state of the economy, radio was flourishing. It had been introduced in the early twenties. In the midst of the Depression, more than 20 million homes had at least one radio.

In the fall of 1932, Reagan hitchhiked to Chicago to start his adventure, going from one radio station to another. At the largest, best-known stations, he received one rejection after another. He wasn't prepared for this setback and almost gave up. After all, he had no contacts, no "ins," and no experience. Finally, a sympathetic receptionist at NBC suggested he would have a much better chance at radio stations in smaller cities. It was excellent advice, and, fortunately, he followed it.

Davenport, Iowa, the smaller town he chose to start with, was located about 60 miles from his hometown. One of the places he stopped was WOC, its call letters signifying "World of Chiropractic." B. J. Palmer of the Palmer School of Chiropractic founded the station, which was located in the same building in Davenport. When Reagan talked to the station manager, Peter MacArthur, it seemed that he had struck out once again. The station had just hired an announcer that very day. As he walked dejectedly back to the elevators, Reagan mumbled about the waning chance of his ever landing a position as a sports announcer. Immediately, MacArthur asked him if he could announce a football game off-the-cuff and make him believe that it was real. This was a breeze for the lifeguard who had entertained innumerable youngsters on the beach with tales of his favorite high school and college games. With a microphone plopped right in front of him, Reagan regaled MacArthur with the details of a Eureka game he had played the previous fall against Western State University. It worked—MacArthur was impressed, and Reagan was hired, first just to broadcast a game in Iowa City for "five dollars and bus fare." He did so well, he was soon hired as a full-time staff announcer.

Reagan's triumph was short-lived. While he knew exactly how to re-create a football game, he didn't know how to deliver commercials or introduce musical recordings—part of his job. When he not only fumbled his lines but also left out an entire advertisement for the local mortuary—a major sponsor of the program—he was fired as fast as he had been hired. Ironically, he was asked to stay on long enough to train his replacement, and in the course of doing so, he told the man about how quickly the job had come and gone. Worried that he might suffer a similar fate, the man went to MacArthur and asked for a contract in order to secure his job—a novelty in that day and age. MacArthur refused to give him that security, and Reagan was soon rehired at $100 a month.

As a radio announcer for World of Chiropractic (WOC) in Davenport, Iowa, Reagan had taken his first step away from small-town life and into the limelight.

Reagan agreed to come back, of course, but on the one condition that the other announcers would give him some tips so he would do better on the air. They did, and their help, together with learning the value of rehearsing, turned Reagan into an excellent announcer within a short time. He also took inspiration from the newly elected Franklin Delano Roosevelt's "Fireside Chats" on the radio. Reagan's new salary was split between the money he sent back home to his parents, payments on his student loan from Eureka, and a tithe for the church in Dixon.

Proving that sometimes a person is definitely in the right place at the right time, soon after Reagan became a regular at WOC, the station consolidated with its bigger sister station WHO in Des Moines, one of the biggest and most powerful radio stations in the country at that time. Reagan moved to this growing city of more than 140,000 people and doubled his salary just in time to help his parents even more. Because Jack had suffered a serious heart attack and could no longer work, Reagan's money was a necessity.

It wasn't long before Reagan attracted a following as a radio announcer. His smooth, warm voice was well suited to radio, and in cities and towns throughout the Midwest, people recognized him as the voice behind the Big Ten football games as well as the announcer of major league baseball. Reagan had another advantage with this new station: Des Moines was a popular place for up-and-coming movie stars to stop for some promotion. During Reagan's time there, he met many actors and actresses, including Leslie Howard and James Cagney.

One of Reagan's favorite stories about his days on radio occurred when he had to learn the true meaning of the word "improvisation." Since Des Moines was quite a distance from where the Chicago Cubs' games were actually being played, the ability to re-create the play-by-play action was a talent. Each play was sent over the telegraph wire, and Reagan's assistant, Curly, had to pass the information through a window to Reagan in the broadcasting booth. He, in turn, would take the information, add fillers here and there, and create the scene for his listeners. In between messages, he would improvise about what different players were doing while an applause record on a turntable, foot-operated by Reagan, backed up each play.

One fateful day, during the ninth inning of a game between the Cubs and the St. Louis Cardinals—a scoreless tie—disaster struck. The wire went dead. For an agonizingly long six minutes and 45 seconds, Reagan improvised on what was happening while he and Curly waited for the wire to start up again. His reporting included an amazing 19 foul balls, as well as a fictional story about a redheaded kid who was scrambling after one of them. This performance brought Reagan "hero" status at the station.

Reagan's social life as a bachelor was surprisingly tame. He spent some time hanging out in bars with his coworkers and fraternity brothers, but he usually preferred to dance than to drink. His father's example had taught him the folly of getting too involved with alcohol. For all his life Reagan would be a very moderate drinker.

While Reagan was at WHO, he had the opportunity once more to help his brother. When Neil was unable to find work, Reagan had him come

As a radio sportscaster in Des Moines, Iowa, Reagan's favorite part of the job was doing the play-by-play for the Chicago Cubs baseball games, even though he could not watch the game. His information came through a telegraph operator, and once, when the line went dead, he made up what was happening for nearly seven minutes!

to Des Moines and move in with him for a while. It wasn't easy for either of them; they had less in common now than they did when they were kids. Neil went to the station with his brother, and one day—while listening to Reagan make his usual predictions about the outcome of upcoming football games—Neil openly disagreed with his brother. Reagan pushed a microphone in front of him, and they bantered back and forth about who was right. MacArthur liked it, and soon Neil was hired to be on air with his brother as well as do some commercials. Within six months, Neil was made program director. Later, he would go on to become director, then producer, network executive, and finally the vice president of a major advertising agency.

After several years, Reagan had enough of radio announcing and decided to pursue his original goal of becoming an actor. In 1937, he went to Catalina Island in California to cover the Chicago Cubs' winter training camp. While there, he wanted to look up some contacts in the movie business. One was an actress and singer he had met in Des Moines named Joy Hodges, and when he confessed that he really wanted to act, she set up an appointment for him with George Ward of the Meiklejohn Agency. After one look at Reagan's handsome, all-American face, Ward knew he had a winner. Calling his boss, he stated that he had the next Robert Taylor in his office.

Meiklejohn arranged for a screen test for Reagan at Burbank's Warner Brothers. It went well—what there was of it. Reagan left for Des Moines the following morning, and in less than 48 hours, received a telegram: Warner was offering him a seven-year contract at $200 a week. Warner Brothers was a powerful studio at that time, producing an average of 60 pictures a year and boasting such stars as Bette Davis, James Cagney, and Spencer Tracy. Reagan's dream was starting to come true.

After a last-minute farewell party in Iowa, Reagan packed his belongings in his Nash and headed for Hollywood. His first day of work was June 1, 1937, and Reagan had a case of stage fright that almost paralyzed him. Just before getting ready to play his first part—that of a small-town radio announcer in *Love Is on the Air*—the studio executives tried to decide what to do about his name. Dutch Reagan just didn't fit. When he suggested Ronald, they approved. Thus, Reagan was identified by his real name instead of his nickname. *Love Is on the Air* was a B picture for Warner Brothers, taking only three weeks to make and costing about $119,000. It received good reviews, however, and Reagan's career as a motion picture actor had begun.

Most of Reagan's parts were either bigger roles in B pictures or smaller parts in A pictures. He was usually cast as a handsome and not very intelligent character, often a newspaper reporter or war hero. He was once referred to as "the Errol Flynn of B pictures." He starred in four films in which he played Lieutenant "Brass" Bancroft, a character inspired by the real-life adventures of a retired U.S. Treasury agent. It was during the filming of one of those movies that he suffered hearing damage in his right ear that would plague him for life, a result of an actor firing a blank .38 caliber cartridge too close to his ear. During his first year in Hollywood, Reagan wrote articles about his impressions of California for the *Des Moines Register*, sharing many of his experiences.

The movie roles continued to roll in, one after another, and after six months, he was making enough money to send for his parents to join him

REAGAN'S FAMILY, TAKE TWO

Jack, Nelle, and Neil were a big part of Reagan's life even after he found success on the silver screen. He bought his parents their first real home and moved them to Hollywood so they could be close to him. Knowing that Jack would feel as if he was being handed charity, Reagan asked him if he would be willing to take a job at the studio helping him handle all of his fan mail. Jack's new job entailed opening letters, reading requests, selecting photos of his famous son, and mailing them to fans.

Jack was settling down into a much steadier routine than he had previously been used to. He worked for his son, had a home that was paid for, and had even returned to the Catholic Church. And he gave up alcohol. Sadly, he had a heart attack at the age of 58. Jack died at home on May 18, 1941.

In her later years, Nelle lived in a nursing home, struck by the same disease that would eventually afflict her sons—Alzheimer's. She died on July 25, 1962, after her son's movie career had shifted from film to television. Her passing was very hard on him; Nelle had been a constant, stabilizing, and loving force in his life for more than 50 years.

Reagan's older brother, Neil, followed in his brother's footsteps for many years. Neil also had a brief career in radio and films, appearing in *Doughboys in Ireland* (1943) and *Tugboat Annie Sails Again* (1940). Afterward, he left acting and became a success in the advertising/marketing business.

Neil married Bess Hoffman. They had no children. Both brothers would develop colon cancer in later life, and then, like their mother, both were diagnosed with Alzheimer's disease. Neil died of heart failure on December 11, 1996, in San Diego, California, at the age of 88.

in California. He found them an apartment, and Nelle immediately settled in by joining a nearby church.

The year 1938 was a hectic one for Reagan. He made nine pictures and was elected a director of SAG, the Screen Actors Guild. He was often seen out on the town with a variety of starlets, including Lana Turner, Mary Jane Crane, and Anita Louise. The following year, his life changed even more dramatically when he met his co-star Jane Wyman on the set of *Brother Rat.* She was in the middle of a divorce, and as soon as it was finalized, Wyman began to date Reagan. Their romance was the talk of every gossip column and magazine. Finally, when the two actors joined Louella Parsons for one of her much-publicized nine-week vaudevillian cross-country tours, the two became engaged. Reagan gave Wyman a 52-karat amethyst engagement ring. On January 26,

Movie fans all over the world enjoyed watching the courtship of Reagan and Jane Wyman. As they officially apply for their wedding license, the sign hides Wyman's amethyst engagement ring.

JANE WYMAN—BEFORE AND AFTER REAGAN

Before that fateful meeting between Wyman and Reagan on the set of *Brother Rat* in 1938, Jane Wyman had been working hard for several years to get a Hollywood career going. Born Sarah Jane Mayfield, her year of birth varies from source to source (somewhere between 1914 and 1917). At first, her movie roles were small ones. It wasn't long, however, before she was noticed in Hollywood. Her dark, expressive eyes and stage presence came through strongly. In 1936, she signed a long-term contract with Warner Brothers under her new name, and soon she was appearing in both A and B films.

Ronald Reagan and Jane Wyman

Wyman had been married twice before she married Reagan. The first time was to a young salesman named Ernest Wyman when she was only 16. The relationship lasted less than two years. Her next marriage was to businessman Myron Futterman. Once again, it was over before the two-year mark, a pattern that Wyman would follow in later life, except in her marriage to Reagan. During their time together, Wyman had some of the biggest movie roles of her career. She was nominated for Best Actress for her portrayal of Ma Baxter in *The Yearling*, and she was awarded an Oscar for her role as a deaf-mute rape victim in *Johnny Belinda*.

After her divorce from Reagan, Wyman married two more times—each marriage lasting two years. Her only children were from her marriage to Reagan: Maureen, who passed away in 2001, and Michael. She continued to act in a series of films, including *Stage Fright*, *The Glass Menagerie*, *Magnificent Obsession*, and *All that Heaven Allows*. From 1955 to 1958, Wyman hosted television's Fireside Theatre, starring in many episodes and acting as co-producer for the series.

How to Commit Marriage (1969) was Wyman's last feature film. She played the role of Angela Channing on the television series *Falcon Crest* from 1981 to 1990 and has been in several made-for-TV movies since then. Each year, Wyman also presents the Jane Wyman Humanitarian Award from the Arthritis Foundation in California.

Reagan played George "The Gipper" Gipp in Knute Rockne—All American *in 1940, starring Pat O'Brien as the famous Notre Dame coach.*

1940, the two were married in the Wee Kirk O'Heather Church in Glendale, California. Their reception was held at the Beverly Hills' home of columnist Louella Parsons. When the couple returned from their honeymoon in Palm Springs, they moved into Wyman's apartment near the famous Sunset Strip.

From the beginning, Wyman and Reagan were considered Hollywood's dream couple. On the surface, things couldn't have been much better for either one of them. Reagan had the chance of a lifetime when he found out that Warner Brothers was making a picture about one of his biggest heroes, Knute Rockne, the coach of the Notre Dame football team. Urged on by his new wife and convinced that he was the only one who could play George Gipp, the running back who dies of pneumonia two weeks after his final game, he sought an audition. Hal Wallis of Warner Brothers, however, refused. He thought Reagan was too lightweight for the part and didn't look much like a football player. To help convince him, Reagan ran home, found a photo of himself in his old football uniform, and dashed back to the studio to show it to Wallis. He won the role, and it became one of his best-known characters. The line from the film in which Rockne tearfully urges his team to "win one for the Gipper" was one that Reagan would later use to motivate voters in his political speeches.

Proud of his work in this film, Reagan brought his father to Indiana for the opening of the film at Notre Dame. Jack was impressed with his son and said how proud he was to be there when he became a star. That moment would mean a lot to Reagan, as Jack passed away shortly afterward.

The early 1940s brought some of Reagan's biggest successes. He starred in films such as *The Santa Fe Trail, Dark Victory,* and—what he considered his finest movie—*Kings Row,* which was based on the book by Henry Bellamann. In this film, Reagan played a man who just had his legs amputated by a sadistic surgeon. He practiced for weeks with friends, doing the part in front of the mirror and while lying in bed at night. He even took the time to interview physicians and psychologists about what this character would be feeling. Reagan mastered the scene so well that it needed only one take. The anguished line that he said to his co-star Ann Sheridan—"Where's the rest of me?"—meant so much to

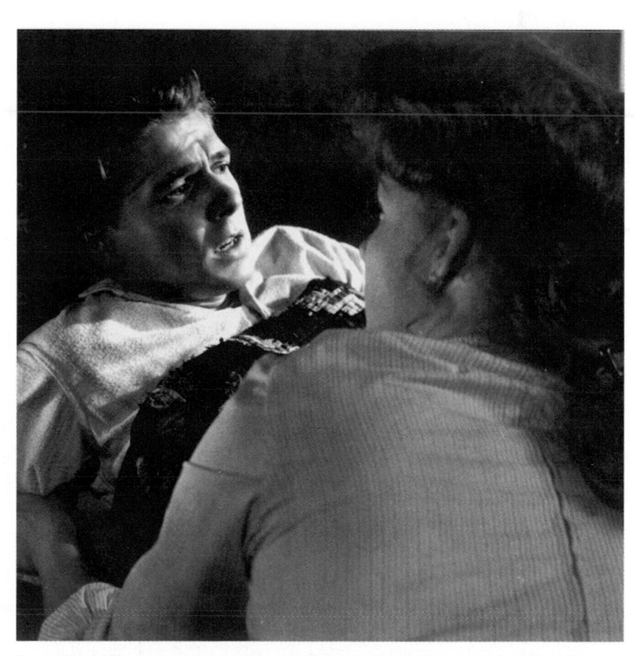

In what Reagan would always consider his best role, he wakes to find that his legs have been amputated. His hoarse cry of "Where's the rest of me?" from Kings Row *was so perfect that the scene was filmed in one "take."*

The year 1941 brought the perfect New Year's gift to the Reagans—their first child, a daughter they named Maureen. As an adult, she would one day follow in her father's footsteps and become a politician.

Reagan that he used it for the title of his future autobiography.

Reagan and Wyman starred in several movies together during these years, including *Brother Rat*, *Brother Rat and a Baby*, *An Angel from Texas*, and *Tugboat Annie Sails Again*. Wyman was very career oriented and focused a great deal of her attention on acquiring the best roles for herself and for her husband. Although rough days were ahead for this golden couple, they still welcomed a baby daughter, Maureen, born on January 4, 1941.

Months later, the Japanese attacked Pearl Harbor, and war became a part of everyone's reality. Even movie stars were not exempt. In April 1942, Reagan entered active duty in the Army as a second lieutenant. He reported to Fort Mason in San Francisco, but due to his poor eyesight, was not qualified for combat duty. Instead, he was assigned to be part of the motion picture unit that created more than 400 training films as well as organized USO tours and other morale boosting activities. Reagan rose to the rank of captain. While he was in the Army, his salary from Warner Brothers stopped, and all he had was Army pay. Knowing that his mother needed the money he sent her on a regular basis, Reagan took out a loan from the studio. At one point, Reagan was allowed a leave of absence from the service so that he could film *This Is the Army*, a joint production between Warner Brothers and the War Department. Profits went to the Army Emergency Relief.

While time in the Army did not hurt Reagan in any physical way, it had definite repercussions on his acting opportunities. Before being called to active duty, he had reached the pinnacle of his acting career, starring in serious films and rating 9 percentage points in popularity above veteran James Cagney. For a time, he received more fan mail than any other actor. He was considered the top box office draw at the time and had even been up for a main role in the upcoming film *Casablanca*, but the war made this impossible. The key roles went to Humphrey Bogart and Paul Heinreid. When Reagan was discharged in the fall of 1945, the situation was quite different for the Reagans. Wyman was now the one who was cast in roles of a lifetime in such

For his entire life, Reagan would credit his mother, Nelle, pictured here with him, for giving him the faith, strength, and conviction to always try to do what is right. She instilled a strong religious faith in her son that would deepen with time.

The Reagan family—Ronald, Jane, Maureen, and Michael

films as *The Lost Weekend*, *The Yearling*, and *Johnny Belinda*, in which she won an Oscar for Best Actress. Reagan, on the other hand, was not offered the same caliber of parts that he was before he went to war. While he had just signed a million dollar contract with Warner Brothers, he was back to playing in a variety of B pictures. This difference had put a wedge between the couple. Even as they adopted their son Michael in March 1945 (Wyman didn't want to take time off for a pregnancy), trouble was brewing. Reagan's slow-growing interest in politics made the wedge grow wider. Wyman had no interest in being married to a politician—she had married a movie star.

Reagan was elected president of the Screen Actors Guild in 1947, a position he would hold through 1952. His tenure only intensified his interests in politics. He learned the art of negotiation by working on various contracts, and through this new skill he developed one of the principles that would stay with him throughout his years in office. When he was faced with making big decisions for many people, he finally decided that the only way he could do it and still sleep at night was to always do what he honestly and internally felt was right, whether or not it was the popular choice.

In June 1947, Wyman gave birth to a three-month, premature daughter named Christine. Meanwhile, because Reagan was in the hospital with a serious case of viral pneumonia, she was left to go through the experience alone. After Christine died nine hours after she was born, the couple drifted even further apart. Finally, in 1948, after eight years of marriage, Reagan came home to find the house empty and Wyman and the children's belongings gone. Although he knew they had some problems, he hadn't considered the possibility of divorce. The reason Wyman listed on her divorce papers was the umbrella one, "mental cruelty."

Occasional appearances at some of the same Hollywood gatherings would always spark rumors of reconciliation, but there was never really any chance of that happening. For months, Reagan was lost, not sure how to go on without Wyman. Throughout the innumerable interviews, articles, and books that Reagan would do in later years, he avoided discussing his marriage to Wyman. He always refused to say exactly what it was that caused the divorce, only commenting that he was sorry for the pain it caused Maureen and Michael. Wyman was often quoted as saying it was Reagan's passion for politics that ended the marriage. It was a quick, no-contest divorce in which Wyman received full custody of both children.

The next few years were hard ones for Reagan. Several of his last films had brought some of his harshest reviews, especially the

Actors, members of SAG, discuss a film strike. From left to right, Jane Wyman, Henry Fonda, Ronald Reagan, and Boris Karloff.

doomed *That Hagen Girl* with the grown-up Shirley Temple. In late 1948 and early 1949, he went to Europe to film *The Hasty Heart* with Patricia Neal. It was a long, dreary, wet experience full of delays and disappointments for Reagan. One thing he did to fill the empty moments between scenes was study British politics, and he would spend time in the local bar discussing issues with anyone who would listen.

In the fall of 1949, while playing in a charity baseball game for the City of Hope research hospital, Reagan was tripped as he slid into first base, breaking his leg in four places. The injury was so serious that he was immobilized in the hospital for almost two months, was on crutches for weeks after that, and would limp for another year. He lost out on two movie roles during the time he was out of commission, losing approximately $150,000 in the process.

Subsequently, Reagan took the role of the professor in the movie *Bedtime for Bonzo.* Although it was a warm and entertaining film, it

When Reagan made Bedtime for Bonzo *in 1951, he thought he was just doing a light-hearted comedy. Little did he know how many times that movie would come back to haunt him during his political career. He is pictured here with his co-star Diana Lynn.*

Reagan (left) plays the Hall-of-Fame pitcher Grover Cleveland Alexander in the 1952 film The Winning Team, *with Wayne Morris (center) and an unidentified actor.*

would elicit many jokes during his later political campaigns. For the next year, he was unemployed. In December 1950, he appeared on television for the first time, starring in the *Nash Airflyte Theatre*.

In 1951, Reagan made his last film for Warner Brothers. *The Winning Team,* another sports story, portraying the life of Grover Cleveland Alexander—one of the greatest pitchers of all time—who played for the St. Louis Cardinals. When Reagan's contract came up for renewal, Warner Brothers chose to let it lapse. On January 28, 1952, Reagan left the Warner lot for the last time, ending a 15-year period in which he had made 53 films. Now he had the time he wanted to immerse himself in more political endeavors, including his work with SAG.

As Reagan entered his forties, he had little idea of all that would lie ahead. His days in the spotlight weren't over. Instead, they would shift to the new medium of television. While the spotlight in Reagan's life tended to fade now and then, it never went out; it would remain on him for the rest of his life.

Back to living the bachelor life, Reagan also could not have guessed that the lasting love of his life was just around the corner, waiting for fate to bring them together. A great deal of his future would be found in a petite and little-known actress named Nancy Davis, a woman whom Reagan would always refer to as "the person who saved my soul."[1]

[1]Nancy Reagan (introduction by William F. Buckley, Jr.), *Ronald Reagan: An American Hero,* 98.

CHAPTER FIVE

SEIZING A GREATER ROLE

Change comes swiftly, bringing Reagan a new career, a new wife, and a new direction in life.

The next decade of Reagan's life would bring about personal and professional changes that would put him on an entirely different journey through life than the one he had been taking thus far. Fame and fortune would still be there, but through a very different field and with a different partner by his side.

The 1950s were a volatile time in Hollywood. anticommunist feelings were running high, and the House Un-American Activities Committee (HUAC) was taking a serious look at the entertainment world, suspicious that Communists were using it as a vehicle to subtly introduce their concepts. Actors, producers, and directors in the field of filmmaking were being questioned, and the names of those suspected were being compiled.

Because of his growing interest in politics and his leadership roles in Hollywood, Reagan soon found himself embroiled in this issue. He testified before the HUAC, sharing its concern about the effort of Communists to infiltrate some Hollywood labor unions. Although he took some criticism from his peers for his participation in the HUAC, he also worked, through his position in SAG, to help clear the names of people who had been falsely accused of Communist activities. One of the people he helped clear would turn out to be the one he would spend the rest of his life with—an actress named Nancy Davis.

During this period in Hollywood's history, actors and actresses made sure to keep their names as clear from potential rumor as possible so as not to run the risk of being "blacklisted." When newcomer Nancy Davis received mail from some left-wing radical groups, she realized that somehow her name had made it onto a list of Communist sympathizers. Concerned, she contacted Mervyn LeRoy, a director, and asked how to clear her name. He suggested that she contact the current SAG president, Ronald Reagan.

Learning the art of grace under pressure, Reagan testifies in front of the House Un-American Activities Committee in the fall of 1947. While he made his anticommunist feelings clear, he never named a single name, even though he was pressured to do so.

Nancy Davis Reagan

Nancy had met Reagan at a party just a few months ago and remembered what a handsome, charming man he seemed to be. She telephoned him, and even though he reassured her that he had already checked into it and her name was clear, the two decided to meet over dinner to discuss it further. Later they would both chuckle over the fact that each was fibbing when telling the other one it would have to be an early night because of a casting call the next morning. Reagan was still hurting from his divorce from Jane Wyman.

Still walking on canes from his baseball accident, Reagan had dinner with Nancy, and before they knew it, they had agreed to extend the evening by going to a nightclub to hear Sophie Tucker and Xavier Cugat's band. They stayed for the second show, not leaving until 3 A.M., when the club closed. Reagan found himself talking about everything from his beloved ranch and his love of horses to his political leanings and work at SAG. He found an eager and interested listener in Nancy, who began attending SAG meetings regularly and listening to his speeches.

Reagan was also making extra cash by appearing in some pictures for several other studios and starring in a number of magazine advertisements. In 1953, for example, he modeled the wrinkle-free collar for Van Heusen Century Shirts.

Although both Reagan and Nancy continued to date other people for more than two years, by February of 1952 he knew he wanted to have Nancy at his side for all of the years ahead. "And one night over dinner as we sat at a table for two, I said, 'Let's get married.' She deserved a more romantic proposal than that, but—bless her—she put her hand on mine, looked into my eyes, and said, 'Let's.'"[1]

On March 4, 1952, Reagan married Nancy Davis, the woman he would love for the rest of his life. To the right of the couple are Ardis and William Holden.

[1] Taken from the "Hollywood" section of Ronald Reagan's official Internet site, http://www.ronaldreagan.com/hollywood.html.

On March 4, 1952, Nancy Davis, 30, and Ronald Reagan, 41, were married at the Little Brown Church in Studio City, California. Their best man was actor William Holden, and his wife, Ardis, was Nancy's matron of honor. Their wedding night was spent at the Old Mission Inn in Riverside, and the honeymoon was a visit to Phoenix, Arizona, where Reagan could—at long last—meet Nancy's parents, Edith and Loyal Davis. Dr. Davis would be an influential person in Reagan's later political life, introducing him to many thoughts and perspectives that would contribute to Reagan's eventual swing to the right.

In October of the same year, the Reagans welcomed their first child, a daughter named Patricia Ann. Reagan began to call his wife "mommy" after she had Patti but changed it to "honey" when he entered the political arena. Although Patti would—years later—write an autobiography that frequently portrayed her parents in a negative light, she also had to admit that they had an intensely close romantic relationship, sometimes stating that they were like two halves of a circle and were complete only when put together. Reagan would often liken coming home to his wife to coming out of the cold into a warm, fire-lit room.

The first few years of marriage were rather lean ones as Reagan struggled to find work. He believed his years as president of SAG had hurt his career. Studios, he thought, now saw him as someone they had to negotiate terms with across a table rather than as a talented actor. In 1953, in an effort to make a little extra income, he even sent out postcards to his long list of fans, offering to sell them autographed photos: a quarter for an eight by ten; a dime for a five by seven.

In early 1954, Reagan agreed to do a two-week engagement at The Last Frontier nightclub in Las Vegas for $30,000. This was a new experience for him and one that he would swear never to repeat. He was hired to be the master of ceremonies for a typical variety show, with singers, dancers, and a comedy troupe. He told jokes, introduced acts, and even performed in a few skits. Although the engagement was a successful one, it was an uncomfortable role for Reagan and one that made him rethink his career. He started to set his sights in another direction—one that was getting the attention of the entire country.

In postwar America, a new form of entertainment—television—had come along that, despite the predictions of some naysayers, was sweeping the nation. In 1953, Reagan appeared seven times on TV dramas such as *Schlitz Playhouse of the Stars*, *Ford Theatre*, and *Kraft Suspense Theatre*. Reagan discovered that, despite Hollywood's disdain for this new medium, it worked quite well for him. One of the other people to recognize this match was the head of Music Corporation's Revue Products, Taft Schreiber. In 1954, he had a proposal for Reagan that would not only take care of the family's finances and provide more acting opportunities for Reagan, but would coincidentally also give him some of the skills he would later put to use as he entered politics.

Schreiber wanted Reagan to be the regular host of the new television series, *GE Theatre Presents*, airing each Sunday evening on CBS. For $125,000 a year (later raised to $150,000), Reagan was to introduce and close each episode and to act in some of them. Each time he took a role, he would receive a bonus. This show would help launch the television careers of many prestigious actors, such as Bette Davis and Joan Crawford. Reagan's role as host of the series was an unqualified success. In his first season, the show was 19th in the ratings; the following year, it was 10th and in the next, it was 3rd. It held the number one slot for Sunday evening programming for years—until the hour-long colorized *Bonanza* aired on another channel and took away its high ranking.

Reagan's duties for GE, however, didn't end there. In a shrewd business decision, GE also expected Reagan to be their overall spokesperson, traveling to their 135 factories and offices throughout the United States to give speeches, promote products, and increase the morale of GE employees and executives. Each visit would be an additional bonus to his usual salary. Reagan was expected to help explain management policies to the labor force. In many ways, these presentations acted as a hands-on political apprenticeship for him. He learned to pay close attention to how he paced his words, altered his

A Christmas photo of the Reagan family.

NANCY DAVIS REAGAN

Nancy Davis was born Anne Frances Robbins. She was not the typical movie star of the 1950s. She didn't arrive in Hollywood until she was 28, and when she did, she usually found herself playing wholesome mothers and wives. Unlike many who yearned for the spotlight and Oscar nominations, her greatest ambition in life was to have a good marriage.

Nancy's father, an auto salesman, abandoned his wife, Edith Luckett, soon after Nancy was born. Edith was also an actress, and she spent much of Nancy's early years on the road, touring the country for various stage and radio jobs. Nancy spent a lonely childhood, but when she was a teenager, her mother remarried and things changed dramatically. Her new stepfather was the well-known Chicago surgeon, Dr. Loyal Davis, who promptly adopted his new stepdaughter. Edith quit the theater to be a wife and mother, but when she saw Nancy's growing interest in acting, she encouraged her to pursue it.

Nancy attended Smith College, where she performed in a number of plays. After she graduated, Edith introduced her daughter to Spencer Tracy. He arranged for Nancy to have a screen test at MGM, and in 1949, she signed a contract with the studio. Between 1949 and 1957, she would make 11 films for MGM, including the starring role in *The Next Voice You Hear* in 1950. When her contract came up for renewal, however, MGM chose to let her go. That was all right with Nancy, who, by the end of her contract, was Mrs. Ronald Reagan. She had achieved her life's goal, and one day her marriage would be considered one of the strongest and most dedicated in America.

As a spokesperson for General Electric, Reagan not only entertained people on television with the weekly show General Electric Theatre *but also toured the country giving speeches, meeting people, and listening to their concerns. All of it proved to be a fabulous practice run for what was waiting for him down the road.*

voice, and paused for maximum effect. He found it was most effective to make brief opening remarks about values and problems and then take questions. Often he would clip out news stories from the local newspaper and incorporate the information into his presentation. His notes were written on index cards in his own personal shorthand, and his ability to read and memorize information quickly—as he had done in school—came in handy once again.

All of these techniques were ones that Reagan would one day use in his presentations as both governor and president. In the eight years he worked with GE, Reagan would speak to more than 250,000 employees, sometimes doing as many as a dozen or more talks in a single day. In addition to his GE appearances, he was also in demand as a speaker by organizations such as the Kiwanis, Lions, Rotary, and chambers of commerce. He was a popular speaker wherever he went. All of this travel was done by train, for Reagan had a long-time aversion to flying. He was on the road for weeks on end, leaving Nancy and Patti at home. Most stops included a banquet somewhere, and Reagan often referred to these trips as "the mashed potato circuit." All in all, this part of his job with GE turned out to be an important prelude to his political development. It was the perfect opportunity for him to improve his speaking techniques without the public scrutiny and media dissection that his political speeches would one day undergo.

After his second year with the company, the Reagans received an unusual bonus. When the Reagans built a new house in the Pacific Palisades section of Los Angeles, GE equipped it with state-of-the-art electrical appliances, including then-new conveniences such as garbage disposals, dimmer switches, and recessed ceiling lights. While with GE, Reagan also did two promotional record albums for them. "Ronald Reagan Recommends" records featured a dozen songs that he would introduce, eight of them Academy Award winners.

In the beginning, Reagan's speeches to the GE workers were based on stories from his Hollywood years, plus information about various GE products and ideas. As time went by, and after listening to the questions and concerns of the employees, his speeches took on a more political tone. Frequent topics included attacks on government-sponsored medical care for the elderly (later known as Medicare) and income tax, as well as support for the concept of a voluntary, rather than mandatory, social security program.

For the most part, GE didn't object to Reagan's increased focus on politics, but in 1959 that changed. In a speech about wasteful government spending, Reagan included the Tennessee Valley Authority (TVA) as an example. The TVA was a $50-million-a-year customer of GE. Reagan agreed to drop TVA from his speeches. Three years later, however, when Reagan's contract with GE was up for renewal, they made a serious request of him. They wanted him to keep politics completely out of his presentations and to focus instead on selling their products. Reagan refused—and so his contract

REAGAN'S FILMOGRAPHY FROM 1937 TO 1964

1937 *Love Is on the Air**
1938 *Hollywood Hotel**
*Swing Your Lady**
*Sergeant Murphy**
*Accidents Will Happen**
*Cowboy from Brooklyn**
*Boy Meets Girl**
*Girls on Probation**
*Brother Rat**
1939 *Going Places**
*Secret Service of the Air**
*Code of the Secret Service**
*Naughty But Nice**
*Hell's Kitchen**
*The Angels Wash Their Faces**
*Smashing the Money Ring**
*Dark Victory**
1940 *Brother Rat and a Baby**
*An Angel from Texas**
*Murder in the Air**
*Knute Rockne All American**
*Tugboat Annie Sails Again**
*Santa Fe Trail**
1941 *The Bad Man***
*Million Dollar Baby**
*Nine Lives Are Not Enough**
*International Squadron**
1942 *Kings Row**
*Juke Girl**
*Desperate Journey**
1943 *This Is the Army**
The Rear Gunner
For God and Country
Jap Zero
1945 *Target Tokyo*
The Fight for the Sky
1947 *Stallion Road**
*That Hagen Girl**
*The Voice of the Turtle**
1949 *John Loves Mary**
*Night Unto Night**
*The Girl from Jones Beach**
*It's a Great Feeling**
1950 *The Hasty Heart**
*Louisa****
1951 *Storm Warning**
*The Last Outpost*****
*Bedtime for Bonzo****
*Hong Kong*****
1952 *She's Working Her Way through College**
*The Winning Team**
1953 *Tropic Zone*****
*Law and Order****
1954 *Prisoner of War***
*Cattle Queen of Montana******
1955 *Tennessee's Partner******
1957 *Hellcats of the Navy*******
1964 *The Killers****

* denotes Warner Brothers
** denotes MGM
*** denotes Universal
**** denotes Paramount
***** denotes RKO
******denotes Columbia
******* denotes Universal Artists

was dropped. His last show was broadcast on September 16, 1962.

During his days with GE, Reagan made a few movies, including the only one he ever made with Nancy, *Hellcats of the Navy*. He played a World War II submarine commander in a role that didn't require much acting. Nancy played a nurse who was in love with him. In November 1959, he was also elected to his sixth term as president of SAG just as the group was on the verge of its first strike. As television grew in popularity, fewer people were going to the movies, preferring to stay at home to watch TV.

Television stations were clamoring for copies of old films to broadcast, and studios were happy to sell them to the stations—but without any compensation for the actors who originally made them. Actors believed this was unfair. They also wanted some of the job benefits of other occupations, such things as pensions and medical plans. In a united effort to show their intent, SAG actors walked off stages at every studio, and stayed away for six weeks.

Reagan led the negotiations for SAG, and in one of his tougher battles, managed to do what he did well—help everyone come to an agreement. Studios agreed to pay residuals to the actors and begin basic benefits. For many in Hollywood, he was a real hero. Following the strike, Reagan resigned as the president, and later, he and Nancy both resigned from the SAG board.

Six years after they were married, the Reagans welcomed a second child, this time a son they named Ronald Prescott Reagan and nicknamed "Skipper." At the same time, Michael, the son from Reagan's marriage to Wyman, came to live with them. Maureen was at Immaculate Heart, a Catholic high school on the East Coast. One of the criticisms that would often be leveled at Reagan was that he was a distant father, both emotionally and physically. While he had little problem showing his wife affection in public and private, it was somehow much harder for him to do so with his children. This was most likely due, at least in part, to his experience with his own father. While Jack was an outgoing and outspoken man, he was not an affectionate father. Three

It wasn't difficult for actress Nancy Davis to look lovingly at her co-star Ronald Reagan in their only movie together, Hellcats of the Navy. *She was already his wife and very much in love.*

An early photo of Nancy and Ronald Reagan

In Reagan's last film appearance, he starred with Angie Dickinson in Ernest Hemingway's The Killers. *The nation was shocked to see him portray a nasty villain, a departure from his "good-guy" roles. The film was made for television but was shifted to the theater when censors determined it was too violent to be shown on TV.*

of Ronald Reagan's four children would grow up to write autobiographies that said harsh things about their father. They cited his distance and lack of affection, as well as Nancy's total immersion in her husband, as reasons the children often felt left out. Despite this early alienation, however, each one rallied around their father in later years, and Maureen, who passed away from cancer in 2001, campaigned to raise funds and awareness for the Alzheimer's disease that was stealing her father away.

By the mid 1960s, Reagan's days in acting were almost at an end. Thanks to his eight years with GE, however, finances were no longer an issue for his family. He starred with Angie Dickinson in *The Killers*, a movie originally intended for television. It was so violent, however, that it had to be shown in theaters instead. Audiences were shocked to see Reagan play a villain. Nevertheless, many critics considered it to be one of his best roles.

Reagan's only other job with television was a brief stint as the host of the syndicated western anthology series *Death Valley Days*. In an echo of what happened years ago to the Reagan brothers at WHO, this time it was Neil Reagan who helped his brother find work. Now a vice president at the McCann-Erickson advertising agency, Neil had as a client the U.S. Borax Company, sponsor of *Death Valley Days*. When they were looking for someone to replace the aging host of the show, Neil recommended his brother, and the U.S. Borax Company agreed. During 1965 and 1966, Reagan hosted 21 episodes. His last television appearance as an actor was on one of those episodes. Entitled, "Raid on the San Francisco Mint," Reagan played banker William Chapman Ralston, a man who single-handedly saves the city from financial ruin. At the time it aired, he was running against Pat Brown for governor of California, and his opponent felt it gave him an unfair advantage to be on television in front of voters every week. All in all, Reagan had more than 60 television appearances before he put his acting career behind him.

Until the early 1960s, Reagan had been a Democrat, following his father's footsteps in their mutual distrust of big business and their faith that the government would and should take care of national problems. When Reagan listened to the concerns and worries of the GE workers and other people he met, however, his opinions changed. He worried that government was getting too big and powerful and gaining too much control over people's lives. Although he had been a staunch supporter of Franklin D. Roosevelt in his youth and campaigned for Harry Truman in 1948, he now found himself saying that though he was a Democrat, he agreed with the positions on issues put forth by Republican candidates. In 1952, he campaigned for Republican Dwight Eisenhower. In 1960, he did the same for Richard Nixon. Talks with others—such as his new father-in-law—further swayed Reagan over to the Republican side.

Finally, in the fall of 1962, as he was campaigning one day for Nixon, who was then running for California governor, a deputy registrar of voters in the audience spoke up and asked him if he was still listed as a Democrat, despite the fact that he had a reputation for campaigning for Republicans. When he replied that he was, she came up on stage and announced that she was going to change that. Then and there, Reagan made the official switch to the Republican Party—after more than 30 years as a Democrat. Less than two years later, he would receive a telephone call that would deepen that new allegiance in an important way. Senator Barry Goldwater, the Republican nominee for president, had a campaign that was in trouble, and he was calling to see if Reagan would be willing to help him. It was a critical moment in Reagan's life. He agreed to do it and then made preparations to make a televised speech entitled "A Time for Choosing." Even Reagan didn't realize just how far that "yes" would take him.

Reagan would write two autobiographical books during his lifetime. The first—*Where's the Rest of Me?*—was published in 1965. While the book's title was taken from his most dramatic and memorable line in the film *Kings Row,* it seemed that, when he was in his forties, this question was largely answered. When he met and married Nancy, the first part of him that was missing was found. When he turned away from acting and set his future sights on politics, he didn't realize it, but he had just found the second part that he needed to make him whole.

Reagan meets with workers at a General Electric factory.

CHAPTER SIX

FROM SCRIPTS TO SPEECHES

"A Time for Choosing" grabs a nation's attention, and California gets a new governor.

Senator Barry Goldwater was in trouble. After defeating Nelson Rockefeller for the Republican Party's nomination for president, he was in the middle of a tough battle against the incumbent president, Democrat Lyndon B. Johnson. Johnson was telling the American people that Goldwater's leadership could endanger world peace, and people were listening. Goldwater needed someone whom people knew and respected to speak up for him, and he knew just the person—his friend, Ronald Reagan.

Reagan had been flirting with the idea of a career in politics for some time, but he believed he was too old to be thinking of starting something new. When Goldwater called him and asked if he would do some fundraising through a speech on his behalf, Reagan was happy to help. The two men saw eye-to-eye on a number of topics, including a strong anti-Communist outlook and wariness about a government that threatened to control people's lives.

Taking the speech that he had honed to perfection while on the road with General Electric, Reagan expanded it to a full 30 minutes and titled it, "A Time for Choosing." In it, he talked about his growing concern about the Soviet Union and the need for the Cold War to come to an end. He described how government was trying to take away people's freedoms, and he urged Americans to support Senator Goldwater so these trends could be halted.

Barry Goldwater was first elected to the Senate in 1952 and served several terms as an Arizona senator, becoming known as "Mr. Conservative." In the 1964 presidential election, incumbent Lyndon Johnson decisively defeated him.

The speech was broadcast nationally on NBC Television on October 27, 1964, one week before the election. According to Neil Reagan, it raised $1 million—a huge amount at the time. More than a thousand letters of praise and support immediately poured in. Reagan's speech was not enough for Goldwater to overcome Johnson's lead, but it had the effect of putting Reagan on the national political stage.

Soon after, Holmes Tuttle, a Los Angeles auto dealer and Republican contributor, and some others asked Reagan to think about running for governor of California in the next

Reagan entered the political world when he made his famous speech "A Time for Choosing" in support of Republican Senator Barry Goldwater, who ran for president in 1964. Here Reagan proudly displays a Goldwater ribbon with a smile.

election in 1966. Tuttle and the group, calling themselves the "Friends of Ronald Reagan," felt he stood a good chance of beating two-term incumbent Pat Brown. Reagan's first reaction was to laugh. At 54, he was just about ready to settle down and enjoy retirement with his wife and children. The last thing he was looking for was an entirely new career. An occasional speech or presentation for a political friend was fine—but governor? Not likely.

The Friends of Ronald Reagan kept talking to him, however, and finally, he agreed to go on the road. He made speeches throughout California for six months to gauge people's reactions. If it truly appeared that the people were eager for him to run, he would consider it.

Starting in early 1965, Reagan toured from one end of California to the other—six times in all. When he returned home and met with his supporters, he decided to run. Everywhere he

PAT BROWN

From his youth, Edmund G. "Pat" Brown was a determined person. He was born in San Francisco in 1905. As a child, he sold Liberty Bonds, and as he did, he would yell Patrick Henry's famous words, "Give me liberty or give me death!" Soon, people referred to the enthusiastic youngster as "Pat," and the nickname stuck.

Brown was a lawyer before he entered politics. He went from having his own practice to being San Francisco's district attorney and then state attorney general. A liberal Democrat, he was first elected governor of California in 1958, defeating William Knowland. Four years later he was reelected, beating former Vice President Richard Nixon.

When Brown realized that his opponent in the 1966 election was going to be Ronald Reagan, the man he had watched in the movies, he was relieved. He was sure this race was going to be an easy one. Much of his campaign was based on the notion that Reagan was incompetent because of his acting history. He even went so far as to make a television commercial in which he and a number of children were watching one of Reagan's old films. He turns to the children and mentions that he is running against an actor, pauses, then reminds the class that it was an actor who shot Lincoln. This was a major mistake, and one that would contribute to his defeat in the election.

In 1975, Brown's son, Jerry, followed in his footsteps and became governor of California, serving two terms. Jerry Brown is known for his intriguing political career *and* for his involvement with Zen Buddhism and female celebrities, such as singer Linda Rondstadt. His father, Pat Brown, died in February 1996.

Ronald Reagan and Pat Brown debate during the California gubernatorial race in 1966.

had gone the response was strong—many Californians wanted Reagan to be their next governor. In January 1966, a month shy of his 55th birthday, he declared his candidacy. Thus, for the first time his hat was in the ring, and he was ready to campaign for himself. He easily won the Republican primary in 1966.

Brown thought that his new opponent would be easy to beat. He was not the first, nor was he the last person to underestimate Reagan's charm and ability to lead. The battle between the two men was not pretty; Brown often referred to Reagan as "just" an actor, implying that he was not too bright and was in over his head. One of Brown's accusations was that Reagan was not writing his own speeches but simply reading them—much as he had read scripts in his Hollywood days. To prove him wrong, Reagan stopped using prepared speeches. Instead—taking a leaf from his GE road trips—he made brief opening remarks, then opened each session to questions from the audience.

In September 1966, Reagan faced Brown on television's *Meet the Press*. In the debate, Brown tried again and again to make Reagan appear unprepared and incompetent. Every attempt failed as Reagan's responses were consistently thoughtful and informed. Later, after the votes were counted, Reagan had won the election with a margin of more than one million votes, taking 58 percent of the popular vote to Brown's 42 percent.

Reagan had won the battle, but he had no idea of the struggles that would still be ahead of him once he entered office. It would be a job that tested every one of his skills and taught him new ones. First, he focused on hiring top people from the business world to form his new administration. Doing this would prove both helpful and harmful. New faces brought new ideas and perspectives, but—like Reagan himself—many of the people he hired were new to the world of politics and would be learning right along with the new governor.

Just past midnight on January 2, 1967, Justice Marshall McComb inaugurated Reagan as the 33rd Governor of California. It was a quiet and private ceremony. That was good news for those

Surrounded by some of the biggest names in Hollywood, Reagan and Nancy celebrate his swearing in as California governor on January 5, 1971. From left to right are Frank Sinatra, Reagan, Vicki Carr, Nancy, and Dean Martin, with John Wayne, Jack Benny, and Jimmy Stewart in the back.

As Nancy proudly looks on, California Supreme Court Justice Marshall McComb swears in Reagan as the 33rd governor of California. Reagan's left hand is on the 400-year-old Bible of Padre Junipero Serra, which is held by California Senate Chaplain Wilbur Choy.

who had elected him. The bad news was that the most populous state in the country was in trouble. He quickly learned that the state government was spending a million dollars a *day* more than it was taking in. Somehow, the previous administration had managed to keep this a secret through some creative bookkeeping. It came as a surprise to Reagan when his new transition team informed him that California had a state debt of almost $350 million. He had only two weeks before he was required, under state law, to present a balanced budget to the legislature. It was a staggering responsibility, but Reagan took it on and began making decisions.

Trying to balance a budget is never an easy task, and it was an especially formidable challenge in California's case because the state faced its worst financial crisis since the Depression of the 1930s. A few months later, Reagan was diagnosed with an ulcer—a condition that would be healed many months later, Reagan believed, by the power of his prayers and the prayers of those who cared about him.

Some of Reagan's decisions weren't popular. He instituted a $200-per-semester charge for in-state students in the University of California system (previously, their tuition had been free); a hiring freeze; and a 10-percent budget cut for state agencies. He also had to do the one thing that he personally hated the most—raise taxes. During his Hollywood days, he had been in the 91 percent tax bracket himself and had sworn if he ever got into a position where he could exert some control over taxes, he would do all that he could to lower them. Since he was now in that position, he had little choice but to raise them when faced with the state's deficit. Over the first term, Reagan would undergo a great deal of criticism for the cutbacks he had made. In the end, however, his decisions would serve California well.

In 1968, the budget had a surplus of more than $100 million. When asked what to do with it, Reagan knew the answer—return it to the people. Some of his advisors didn't agree; they suggested that he use it to reinstate some of the budget items he had cut. Instead, Reagan went on television and informed his constituents about the surplus, letting them know it would be returned to them. By the time he left office he had returned more than $5 billion to the taxpayers of California in the form of tax reductions and lower user fees and tolls. Reagan was establishing a reputation for speaking his mind and keeping his word.

The deficit was not the only challenge that Reagan would face as governor of California. He had come into power during an explosive and turbulent time in the nation's history. Many youths of the 1960s were going through an intense phase of questioning the rules, routines, and customs of the culture. The Vietnam War was a major issue for many, with passionate feelings and a growing gap between the youth, who opposed the war, and the older generation, who generally supported it. Much of the unrest in the nation was showing up on college campuses, where students gathered to protest with words, signs, sit-ins, and sometimes violence to make their points. At the University of California's Berkeley campus, for example, the protesters sometimes got out of control. Within one year, the university had experienced eight bombings or attempted bombings, and more than 1,000 sticks of dynamite and 200 firearms had been confiscated.

Reagan, not surprisingly, was a supporter of the government's policy on the Vietnam War. He believed it was necessary to stop the Communists from taking control of Southeast Asia. While he supported anyone's right to protest, he felt that the students often protested in the wrong manner. He disapproved of violence and would often contrast the peaceful student strike he helped lead back during his days at Eureka to the hostility that was occurring on California college campuses. Students often jeered and taunted him when he tried to talk to them. His attempt at mutual respect and nonviolent negotiations did not appeal to them. They would not listen.

Antiwar sentiment increased throughout the nation after the assassination of Robert F. Kennedy in June 1968. He is pictured here with his wife, Ethel, on the left and Jesse Unruh, his campaign manager, on the right. Moments later, he was shot and killed in an adjacent room.

Reagan was a strong supporter of the war in Vietnam and was not popular among his college-age California constituents, who are pictured here marching on Van Ness Avenue in San Francisco in April 1969.

The war issue intensified in 1968 when President Johnson escalated the country's involvement. Outcries swept the nation. In June, Robert Kennedy was assassinated in Los Angeles, and the social climate became even worse. Repercussions were felt in every corner of the United States and were especially loud in California, where Reagan was about to face one of the biggest conflicts he would ever have to handle as governor.

Earlier in 1969, members of Third World Liberation Front had attacked students who were trying to enter the Berkeley campus. Other protesters held student strikes. Reagan didn't hesitate to respond to these actions. He sent in the California Highway Patrol to keep a watchful eye for any signs of additional violence. More than 2,000 protesters reacted by throwing rocks at the police, and when officers sent tear gas canisters into the crowd, students picked them up and threw them back. Rioters charged the police, trampling them underfoot in the process. Soon, a full-scale riot was underway, with one person killed and some 50 police officers injured.

Reagan took control of the situation by sending in 2,500 members of the National Guard, staying on the campus for 17 days. Conservatives across the country cheered this action, which intensified the anger and loathing of the left. This polarization of attitudes would follow Reagan throughout much of his political career. While many people supported, respected, and loved him as a leader, opponents of his policies considered him to be out-of-date and incompetent. Despite this, Reagan continued to search for common ground on which the generations could communicate.

At one meeting between Reagan and the leaders of several different California campus groups, he managed to make one vital point: "... one of them who was the spokesman said to me, 'Governor, it's impossible for you to understand us.' And I tried to pass it off. I said, 'Well, we know more about being young than we do about being old.' And he said, 'No, your generation cannot understand their own sons and daughters.' He said, 'You didn't grow up in an era of computers figuring in seconds what it used to take men years to figure out.' And he went on like that. And usually you only think of the answer after you're gone, but the Lord was good to me. And he talked long enough that I finally interrupted him, and I said, 'Wait a minute. It's true what you said. We didn't grow up, my generation, with those things. We invented them."[1]

During his years as governor, Reagan would have other issues beyond the deficit and campus violence to deal with. Other goals he focused on included cutting spending, reducing the size of the state government, setting up tougher water quality standards, and increasing protection of rape victims. He also was behind the decision to provide Jewish prison inmates with rabbis when wanted and for allowing conjugal visits for some married prisoners. Other measures included vastly expanding the state park system, requiring environmental impact statements on all state public works projects, and establishing tougher smog control standards.

In 1969, Reagan, in effect, stopped the federal government from building the huge Dos Rios dam in Northern California. It saved the Round Valley Indian Reservation and the town of Covelo from being flooded.

Following an assault on the local police at Berkeley by Vietnam War protestors, Reagan called in the National Guard to calm things down. Although it was effective, it did not endear him to the younger generation.

Not all of Reagan's decisions were ones that he, himself, would later agree with. One of the most controversial issues to come up during his terms as governor came at a bad time for Reagan. He had been in this new position for only four months when abortion became a turbulent issue. Although the famous case of *Roe* v. *Wade* was still six years away, California—often ahead of the rest of the nation on issues—was already dealing with it. California State Senator Anthony Beilenson (D) had introduced a bill called the

---

[1]Remarks at a White House Ceremony Commemorating the Bicentennial Year of Air and Space Flight, February 7, 1983 (Reagan was recollecting the incident).

Therapeutic Abortion Act, which attempted to end illegal abortions that were being done poorly or dangerously. This bill would make abortions legal for women who were at physical risk.

On the surface, this bill made sense to Reagan, even though he was opposed to abortion. When he first encountered the bill, he insisted on a number of amendments that would limit the scope of who would be eligible, and Beilenson agreed to them. Still not sure if he should sign the bill, Reagan met with a number of people on both sides of the issue, including a representative from the Roman Catholic Church and his father-in-law, Dr. Loyal Davis, a prominent surgeon who supported the bill. In the end, Reagan signed the bill but regretted doing so because its wording allowed for far more abortions than he had anticipated.

As governor, Reagan also worked to ensure racial equality in state hiring. He appointed a community relations director to work out of the governor's office. The first director, Bob Keyes, an African American, arranged a series of meetings for Reagan with community leaders and representatives in predominantly African American and Hispanic neighborhoods throughout the state. While these meetings were not secret, they were not open to the press so that there could be an open, candid dialogue.

The Reagans spending a relaxing time together in Sacramento.

Reagan visited families and store owners in Southern California Mexican barrios like this one. He would arrive unannounced and spend time talking with the people about what they needed and wanted from their public officials.

As a result of these meetings, Reagan took steps to improve state civil service exam procedures in order to make more job opportunities available to minorities. And, as was happening all over the country, during his two terms he appointed more minority citizens to decision-making positions in state government than all of his predecessors combined. Meanwhile, the Reagans also showed their support and respect for the soldiers who had fought in Vietnam, sponsoring a number of dinners in their home for returned prisoners of war.

Throughout Reagan's ups and downs as governor, Nancy stayed by her husband's side, being his best friend, confidante, partner, and supporter. Nancy had some of her own programs, such as the National Foster Grandparents Program. She believed it was her role to help protect her husband. Since he was good-natured and looked for the best in everyone—as Nelle had once taught him—Nancy took on the role of the more skeptical of the two, especially when it came to personnel. This meant she also gained a reputation that was less than flattering. Instead of being seen as protective and supportive, she was often written about as being stilted and aloof. It was an image with which Ronald Reagan would never agree and that often upset him

In the early days of his governorship, the negative image of Nancy was sharpened when she insisted they move out of the century-old Governor's Mansion. Many saw this as evidence of what they thought was a superior attitude. In April 1967, the family moved to a large, rented home in Sacramento.

In the middle of Reagan's first term, members of the state Republican Party asked him to run for president in the June 1968 primary. He wasn't interested. He was just settling into his job as governor and didn't want to take anything else on at that time. The party convinced him to run as a favorite-son candidate; that way, he would not be elected but could help prevent another disastrous primary fight like that which had occurred in the Goldwater-Rockefeller primary four years earlier. Reagan finally agreed but was unsettled when he arrived at the convention in Miami, Florida, to find that several delegates were backing him. He received a decent number of votes. Because Nixon had the majority, Reagan went to the stage and moved that the delegates vote for Nixon by acclamation. They did so and Reagan was relieved; he was not ready for the presidency.

In 1974, the Ford administration put out feelers about possible high positions for Reagan, anticipating a possible challenge by him in the 1976 election. He turned down each one.

Toward the end of Reagan's first term as governor of California, he decided to run again. This time his opponent was Jesse M. Unruh, the Speaker of the State Assembly. He won that election with 53 percent of the vote and was sworn in on January 5, 1971. Winning two terms in a row was especially impressive, given that the ratio of Democrats to Republicans in California was about three to two.

The focus of his second term was primarily welfare reform. The state was already known as "the welfare capital" of the nation. The number

Although Reagan did not make a serious run for president in 1968, he did attend the Republican National Convention as California's favorite son. This drew a spectacular ovation from the delegates from California.

Ronald Reagan takes the oath of office for his second term as governor of California on January 4, 1971, administered by California Chief Justice Donald Wright.

of people on welfare was increasing at a frightening 40,000 per month, and if it did not stop, California would ultimately be bankrupt. A thorough examination of the state's welfare system by a special task force showed several problems. At that time, the eligibility standards were so lenient that virtually anyone could qualify. People who were employed full-time were getting benefits while others in much more desperate situations were getting nothing at all. Reagan's goal was not to eliminate welfare but to make certain that the right people were getting the benefits of the program. Committees in all 58 counties of the state were established to put pressure on their legislature to clean up the "welfare mess."

One day, Bob Moretti, the liberal Democrat who had succeeded Jesse Unruh as Speaker of the Assembly, came to see Reagan. As Reagan put it, Moretti said, in mock surrender, "Stop those cards and letters; let's negotiate." They did just that. For several weeks, this new welfare program was the focus for Reagan and his administration, and in the end, the legislature passed the "California Welfare Reform Act of 1971," which not only cut annual costs by hundreds of millions of dollars but also raised benefits for the most needy. Instead of increasing at 40,000 per month, under the new welfare program only 8,000 people were added per month. A new initiative was implemented in which welfare recipients who were capable of working were given jobs and job training. In 1973 and 1974, 76,000 people acquired jobs and were taken off welfare. The collaboration was a huge success and was often called Reagan's most important legislative achievement as governor.

Although Reagan was repeatedly asked to run for a third term, he knew he had accomplished the job he had set out to do and was ready to move on. His last day in office was January 5, 1975. Now that he had been in elective office for eight years, he felt he had a much better grasp of what was and was not working in government. Time and again, he had come up against issues as governor that were beyond his control, for they required national solutions. As Reagan contemplated a future in the direction of Washington, many others had the same idea. He received innumerable calls urging him to run for president in the next election in 1976. Although

NIXON RESIGNATION

The Watergate affair of 1972–1974 kept the nation glued to its television sets, waiting to see what would happen next. Five men had been arrested in the summer of 1972 for attempting to break into and bug the offices of the Democratic National Committee at the Watergate office complex. One of them admitted he used to work for the CIA. Another man was a GOP security aide.

Within a matter of months, the story hit front pages all over the world: The Watergate break-in had been directly tied to the presidential reelection efforts of Richard Nixon. In January 1973, former Nixon aides G. Gordon Liddy and James W. McCord, Jr., were convicted of conspiracy, burglary, and wiretapping from the Watergate incident. Five months later, Nixon's top White House staffers H. R. Haldeman and John Ehrlichman resigned over the scandal.

Reagan was a strong supporter of President Richard Nixon even throughout the Watergate scandal that led to Nixon's resignation. Reagan always felt that not all the facts were revealed about what had happened, and later he agreed with President Gerald Ford's decision to pardon Nixon.

Evidence mounted against the president, including testimony from White House Counsel John Dean, who stated he had discussed the Watergate plans with President Nixon more than 35 times. Finally, on August 8, 1974, President Nixon became the first U.S. president to resign. Vice President Gerald Ford assumed the office and later pardoned Nixon of all charges related to Watergate.

Meanwhile, it was a time of insecurity and doubt, even for Reagan, who, like many others, had not anticipated the trouble that would plague the Nixon presidency. As saddened as he was to see one of his friends and colleagues involved in such a controversy, he was also dubious about what he should do next. He had thought about running for president at the end of Nixon's second term, but Nixon's resignation changed that. Should he wait until 1980? He didn't want to split the Republican Party between himself and Gerald Ford; however, he wasn't comfortable with Ford's position on a number of issues, and he was especially concerned that U.S. national defense capabilities were falling behind those of the Soviet Union. Thus, he made his first real bid for the presidency in 1976.

he kept saying he would be busy with his post-gubernatorial activities, he was actively thinking about it.

In November 1974, the Reagans purchased a 688-acre ranch in the mountains north of Santa Barbara. Named Rancho del Cielo ("ranch in the sky") by the Reagans, this place became Reagan's favorite for more than two decades. From 1981–1989 it was the "western White House" whenever the Reagans were there.

In 1975, Reagan spent much of his time on the road making speeches, much as he had done in his General Electric days, and he listened closely to the people, as he had before. Sometimes he would have as many as ten presentations a month. In addition, Reagan had a nationally syndicated newspaper column and a five-day-a-week radio commentary. Ultimately, 350 stations carried the radio program. The more people listened to him, the more they wanted him to run for president. The more they asked, the more he listened. Finally, on November 20, 1975, Reagan announced his candidacy for the Republican presidential nomination in the 1976 election.

Throughout 1975, Reagan had weighed carefully the matter of contesting a sitting Republican president for nomination. Gerald Ford was an "accidental" president, who was a product of Richard Nixon's resignation in August 1974. Nixon had chosen Ford to be his vice president, replacing Spiro Agnew, who had, himself, resigned in disgrace. Thus, Ford was unelected. Reagan, like most Americans, wanted Ford to have an opportunity to succeed. As the months wore on, however, Reagan found himself increasingly at odds with the Ford administration, especially in the matter of national defense. He thought the administration's efforts to control growing inflation (characterized by "Whip Inflation Now!" buttons) were also ineffective.

Some of Reagan's supporters wanted him to start a third party; most simply wanted him to declare his candidacy. He, himself, said the party must proclaim its program "in bold colors, not pale pastels."

The nomination process was hotly contested from the beginning. Ford won the early primaries. Just when it looked as if Reagan's campaign could not continue, he won the North Carolina primary, followed by many others. Going into the Republican National Convention in Kansas City, Missouri, in July, it was neck-and-neck. Ultimately, Ford prevailed, winning 1,187 votes to Reagan's 1,070.

On the last night of the convention, after he had finished his acceptance speech, President Ford did an unprecedented thing; he invited his former competitor to step to the platform to speak to the delegates. Reagan gave a short but impassioned speech about the values and the future of the nation. It brought the audience to its feet, cheering. The Republican party left Kansas City united.

After Ford lost to Jimmy Carter in November, the nation's economic fortunes declined. Interest

The 1976 vote for a Republican presidential candidate was extremely tight. Reagan nearly won, but incumbent Gerald Ford prevailed in the end. Here Reagan steps up to the podium to congratulate Ford, while Nancy smiles from the left and Nelson Rockefeller watches from the right.

rates and inflation continued to rise; an energy crisis crippled the economy; recession hit the country. Reagan, who had resumed his speaking tours, daily radio commentaries, and twice-a-week syndicated newspaper column, found that supporters all over the country were urging him to run again.

In 1978, Reagan made overseas trips to Japan, Taiwan, Hong Kong, Britain, France, and Germany to confer with government, political, media, and academic leaders. He was encouraged by the response to his views.

In 1979, Iranian radicals seized the U.S. embassy in Tehran, holding 55 Americans hostage. President Carter had not found a way to bring them home, despite a daring rescue mission (which ended in failure and death for many of its personnel).

The Iranian government held 52 American hostages for 444 days. Their capture and the botched attempt to rescue them haunted then President Jimmy Carter. It was Carter's negotiations, however, that finally resulted in the release of the hostages. The Americans were freed and sent home the same day that Reagan was sworn in as the new president, and many people thought it was Reagan's influence that had secured their homecoming. Reagan wanted to make certain that the bulk of the credit went to Carter, so he sent Carter to greet the hostages as they landed in Germany.

Reagan permitted an exploratory committee to be formed on his behalf in March 1979. In November, convinced of the depth and breadth of support he would need for another presidential campaign, he announced his candidacy. Before long, half-a-dozen other Republican aspirants entered the contest.

He lost the first round, the Iowa caucuses, to George Bush, but came back strong in New Hampshire, and moved on to a series of victories that ultimately swept the field of competitors. He led a united party at its convention in Detroit in July 1980.

As Reagan prepared for the general election campaign, he believed, more than ever, in the strength and resourcefulness of the American people. He did not view the people as the cause for the country's "malaise." Instead, he viewed the government as the problem. Rely less on government and more on the people, he reasoned, and the nation's pride will be rekindled. Although he knew there would be no "quick-fix" solutions to the problems facing the United States, he believed that persistence would bring results. He summed up his attitude in the statement: "If not us, then who? If not now, then when?"

CHAPTER SEVEN

A TERM OF TRIUMPH AND TRAGEDY

Although a deranged fan leaves a tragic mark on his first term, President Reagan brings hope to a dejected country.

In the campaign of 1980, Carter continually made the same criticisms about Reagan's platform. During one of their first debates, Reagan said, "There you go again." It was a turning point, for it showed Reagan as reasonable, relaxed, and self-confident.

During the course of their second debate, Reagan had the opportunity to close his speech with a statement that struck a chord with a great many Americans. He asked his listeners to ask themselves, "Are you better off today than you were four years ago?" Few people could say yes to that, with inflation, interest rates, and unemployment at all-time highs. That statement, along with the strength of Reagan's presentation and his choice of George Bush as his running mate, swayed the voters. When the ballots were tallied, Reagan had won 50.7 percent of the popular vote and 489 electoral votes to Carter's 41 percent and 44 electoral votes.

A pre-inaugural gala was held at the Capitol Centre in Maryland, hosted and produced by Reagan's longtime friend Frank Sinatra. On the night of the 40th president's inauguration, January 20, 1981, the Reagans would dance at ten separate inaugural balls, and much of the nation celebrated right along with them. During the following weeks, many reporters asked Reagan why he thought he had won the election by such a large margin. He usually attributed this to his view of himself as just another American and the fact that the voters saw him as one of their own.

Reagan took the oath of office on the same day the Iranians released the U.S. hostages, who were now in American airspace. After a grueling 444 days in captivity, they were now returning home. Efforts late in Carter's term had led to this; however, since these two events occurred at the same time, Reagan was often given the credit for their safe return. He asked Carter to go to Germany to meet the freed hostages while he remained in Washington.

The temperature in Washington was unusually mild for January; however, rain threatened. Just as Reagan stepped up to put his hand on his mother's Bible and take the oath, the sun broke through the clouds, shone down directly on him,

Ronald Reagan and George Bush

Ronald and Nancy Reagan dance at the Smithsonian Museum of American History—last stop on a tour of inaugural balls, January 23, 1981.

and stayed there the entire time he spoke. When he was finished, the sun retreated again. It was an omen of good things to come.

Reagan's management approach was to determine what was needed, then find the best people to do it, just as a chief executive officer (CEO) in a large corporation would. He put great trust in his staff, especially in the people at the top—James Baker, his chief of staff; Ed Meese, his counselor; and Michael Deaver, deputy chief of staff, who kept his image strong with the public. Instead of spending endless hours at work, he tried to keep his office hours from nine to five, retiring in the evening to join Nancy to relax and also, as was his custom when he was governor, to read his Oval Office "homework." Weekends were often spent at Camp David and, when possible, at Rancho del Cielo in California, where the couple was happiest.

At 70 years of age, Reagan diffused age as an issue by joking about it, pretending he had been a contemporary of, say, Thomas Jefferson. This good-humored approach, combined with his vigor, drew chuckles from the news media and endeared him to much of the American public, as well.

The focus of Reagan's first term was threefold: cut taxes, limit the growth and

AGES OF PRESIDENTS AT INAUGURATION

1	George Washington	57
2	John Adams	61
3	Thomas Jefferson	57
4	James Madison	57
5	James Monroe	58
6	John Quincy Adams	57
7	Andrew Jackson	61
8	Martin Van Buren	54
9	William Henry Harrison	68
10	John Tyler	51
11	James Knox Polk	49
12	Zachary Taylor	64
13	Millard Fillmore	50
14	Franklin Pierce	48
15	James Buchanan	65
16	Abraham Lincoln	52
17	Andrew Johnson	56
18	Ulysses Simpson Grant	46
19	Rutherford Birchard Hayes	54
20	James Abram Garfield	49
21	Chester Alan Arthur	51
22	Grover Cleveland	47
23	Benjamin Harrison	55
24	Grover Cleveland	55
25	William McKinley	54
26	Theodore Roosevelt	42
27	William Howard Taft	51
28	Woodrow Wilson	56
29	Warren Gamaliel Harding	55
30	Calvin Coolidge	51
31	Herbert Clark Hoover	54
32	Franklin Delano Roosevelt	51
33	Harry S. Truman	60
34	Dwight David Eisenhower	62
35	John Fitzgerald Kennedy	43
36	Lyndon Baines Johnson	55
37	Richard Milhous Nixon	56
38	Gerald Rudolph Ford	61
39	James Earl Carter, Jr.	52
40	**Ronald Wilson Reagan**	**69**
41	George Herbert Walker Bush	64
42	William Jefferson Clinton	47
43	George Walker Bush	54

influence of government, and rebuild the nation's defense strength. In domestic issues, it was similar to the agenda that he had as governor, but this time he had a foreign and defense policy and would assert it on the world stage.

For several years before his election as president, Reagan had campaigned for "supply-side" tax policies. The theory behind them was that the more you tax something, the less of it there will be to tax. Economist Arthur Laffer had diagrammed this on a napkin one day, showing what came to be known as "The Laffer Curve."

Backed by Laffer and many other economists, Reagan reasoned that if you lowered "marginal" tax rates (that is, the tax on the highest dollar a person made), the money saved by the taxpayer would be invested or spent. The volume of new investments generated would provide more capital for business to expand, which meant hiring more workers to fill new jobs and buying more equipment to operate the expanded factories.

The validity of his argument was supported by history. In the twenties, under President Coolidge, and the early sixties, under President Kennedy, across-the-board, "supply-side" tax cuts had been enacted, resulting in substantial economic growth and, along with it, increased revenue to the U.S. Treasury as a result of the increased economic activity.

Reagan campaigned on the importance of enacting across-the-board tax cuts. Soon after taking office, he proposed this to Congress. Every taxpayer would get a reduction in tax rates, and the lower-income groups would be dropped altogether from having to pay any income tax.

With unified Republican support in the House of Representatives and the votes of "Boll Weevil" Democrats, the tax plan passed, then passed the Senate. Reagan personally campaigned for the program with dozens of lawmakers. He signed the bill at Rancho del Cielo in August 1981, a little over six months after taking office. In its final form, the bill gave all taxpayers a 25 percent reduction over three years.

Using the prevailing method of projecting income and expenses, his administration had forecasted that the total package of tax reductions would result in a comparable loss in revenue to the Treasury. This method of projection is called "static analysis." It assumes that every dollar of reduced taxes will be lost to the economy, more or less forever. Reagan knew, of course, that in reality people would invest, save, and spend the additional money they would have as a result of the tax-cut program.

Not long after his program passed but before it could really take effect, the nation slid into recession (a lagging indicator, as always, resulting from actions taken quite some time beforehand). By November 1992, about a decade later, the tax-cut program's effects were felt, inflation was wrestled sharply down, and the nation entered what would become the largest, longest economic expansion in its history.

In his campaign Reagan had called for a dramatic rebuilding of the nation's defenses. He called it "Peace Through Strength." This program began as soon as he took office. He warned that we would have to spend "whatever it took" to achieve the aim of making sure no one (meaning the Soviet Union) would ever be stronger than the United States.

For two or three years in the middle of Reagan's White House years, the nation's deficit was larger than was deemed historically sustainable. His political opponents blamed the tax program for this. In reality, it was a combination of increased defense spending—which Reagan warned would be necessary—and the failure of the House of Representatives, controlled by the other party, to follow through on promised cuts in other programs.

During the tense months before the tax-cut program could become fully effective and while the country was suffering its way through a recession, Reagan urged his fellow citizens to "stay the course." They did and the results justified their faith. Indeed, polls at the time showed two-thirds of the people were behind his plan.

The Treasury, rather than suffering a projected reduction in revenue, gained hundreds of millions of new dollars from the increased economic activity generated by the tax-cut program and reduced inflation.

Neither media nor political critics seemed able to lay a glove on Reagan. His popularity, assertive leadership, and affable personality all served to make him seem "Teflon-coated." This was not true for Nancy Reagan. Critics jumped on her for redecorating the White House. Eventually she would spend more than $1 million, including 220 new china place settings at $1,000 each. For this expenditure, she would receive considerable criticism, despite the fact that all of the new furniture either came out of government storage or was paid for by money from private contributors. The Knapp Foundation bought the 4,372 pieces of china, which were then donated to the White House. Other people criticized Nancy for her expensive taste in gowns and worried that this new First Lady put too much focus on luxury and wealth. What many did not realize was that the outfits they were criticizing were usually lent by designers in return for the publicity it would provide for them.

In 1980, First Lady Nancy Reagan paid a campaign visit to New York's Daytop Village, a therapeutic community for drug recovery. She was stunned by this glimpse into the nation's drug problem, but she was also impressed by the progress she saw in this community. Soon after, Nancy focused on fighting drug and alcohol abuse across the country, especially among young children. Over the next eight years, her "Just Say No" to drugs crusade included visits to 65 cities in 33 states, in addition to the Vatican and eight foreign countries.

In 1982, Nancy turned media criticism into good-natured laughter when she sang "Secondhand Rose" at the annual Gridiron dinner. She was clad in cast-offs.

While her Foster Grandparent Program and the new "Just Say No" anti-drug program garnered her support, over her husband's two terms in the White House, Nancy would continue to have stubbornly high disapproval ratings in opinion polls.

Despite the negative press, the relationship between Reagan and his wife only deepened throughout his presidency. Nancy had a reputation for asking insightful questions of the people around her husband. She continued the role that she had as governor's wife, looking out for her husband and keeping him as safe as possible. If she did not like how one of his aides or other staff was performing, she did not hesitate to voice her opinion. In future years, when Reagan's health would fail, Nancy would also take on the dedicated—and strenuous—role of caregiver. Her devoted care of Reagan in his last years with Alzheimer's would end up changing her image with the American people a great deal, as they came to respect and admire her.

Although the economy was Reagan's main issue, he was barely given a chance to focus on it before an event occurred that nearly took his life. It seized the public's attention and dramatically intensified Reagan's spiritual faith.

On March 30, 1981, Reagan gave a luncheon speech to the Building Trades Council of the AFL-CIO at the Washington Hilton Hotel. The large audience had passed through metal detectors before assembling for lunch. On leaving the hall, Reagan had to walk 30 feet from the hotel's back entrance to his limousine. A small crowd of spectators had gathered by that entrance. Among them was John Hinckley, Jr., 25. He had a gun, and Reagan was the target.

Reagan waved to the crowd just as six shots rang out, making popping noises. "What the hell was that?" Reagan asked Jerry Parr, head of his Secret Service unit.

In recent months, Hinckley had become obsessed with the movie *Taxi Driver* and its

John W. Hinckley, Jr., was the son of a Denver oil executive. Obsessed with actress Jodie Foster, he shot Reagan in an imitation of a character he had seen in the film Taxi Driver. *He was 25 at the time of the shooting. On June 21, 1982, he was found not guilty by reason of insanity and placed in St. Elizabeth's Mental Hospital in Washington, D.C., where he remains today.*

into the backseat of the limousine, tumbling in on top of him. As he landed on Reagan, the president felt a sharp pain and thought Parr's weight had broken his rib. When he found that he could not breathe well, he wondered whether perhaps the rib had punctured his lung.

The limousine headed for the White House. No one—including the president himself—thought he had been shot. When Parr realized that Reagan was having trouble breathing and was coughing blood, he directed the driver to the nearest hospital, at The George Washington University. When they arrived, Reagan insisted on entering the hospital on his own. He wanted to reassure the American people that he was still capable. He buttoned his suit jacket and with dignity walked through the emergency room doors. Just as he got through them, however, he fell to one knee and was put on a stretcher. His agents thought he had suffered a heart attack. It wasn't until the medical personnel cut off his clothes that everyone realized what had happened. Reagan didn't have a broken rib or suffer a cardiac arrest; he had been shot.

main character, Travis Bickle, as well as an actress in the film, Jodie Foster. Hinckley imitated the Bickle character, including purchasing weapons and stalking a president. His original choice had been Jimmy Carter, but by the time he was ready, Reagan was president. He was sure that his act of violence would charm actress Foster into liking him. Most of Hinckley's Devastator bullets, known for their ability to explode on impact, found human targets. One hit White House Press Secretary Jim Brady in the head, causing brain damage and sending him to a wheelchair for the rest of his life. Secret Service Agent Timothy McCarthy was shot in the chest, and Washington police officer Thomas Delehanty was hit in the neck.

In the chaos that followed, Secret Service Agent Parr didn't answer Reagan's question, but pushed him

Reagan waves as he leaves the Washington, D.C., Hilton just before he was shot by John Hinckley, Jr., in an assassination attempt.

The moments following the shooting on March 30, 1981, were chaotic. Press Secretary James S. Brady was struck in the head, permanently injuring him. At the time of this photo, other agents have already captured the shooter, and Reagan is on his way to the hospital, as yet unaware he has been shot.

One of John Hinckley's bullets had hit the side of the limousine and a slice of the bullet entered Reagan's body under the left armpit. It lodged itself in his lower left lung, a precarious inch from his heart. His lung had collapsed, and he was losing blood. Within a few minutes, Reagan was whisked into surgery for removal of the bullet. Before he was taken to the operating room, however, Nancy, who had been rushed to the hospital as soon as she was told there was a shooting, was at his side.

Throughout the entire ordeal, Reagan maintained both courage and a sense of humor. When he first saw Nancy, he murmured, "Honey, I forgot to duck." In the operating room, he said to the physician, "I hope you're a Republican." He was assured that all hospital personnel, at least for that moment, were, indeed, Republicans. In recovery, he smiled as a nurse took his hand and asked her, "Does Nancy know about us?" His demonstration of grace under pressure impressed the American people more than any speech or action he had ever made. Few realized how close the president had come to dying that day. A few days after his open-chest surgery, he developed an infection and high fever, but antibiotics kept them under control.

This traumatic experience deepened his faith. He felt that the assassination attempt was another part of God's plan. He wrote in his diary, "Whatever happens now I owe my life to God and will try to serve Him in every way I can."

The near-fatal attack changed security arrangements at his public events. No longer would he be able to wade into crowds to shake hands as he had done in the past. This would keep him safer—but prevent him from making the personal contact he so enjoyed.

The president made an amazing recovery from this close brush with death. He did not want the American people to feel that he was permanently impaired from the shooting in any way. Twelve days after being shot, he walked, unaided, into the White House. On April 28, less than a month after nearly dying, he addressed a joint session of Congress to present his economic recovery plan. He received a sustained ovation. He later joked, "That reception was almost worth getting shot for."

THE APPOINTMENT OF SANDRA DAY O'CONNOR

One of the qualities that made Reagan such a popular president was that he kept his word, whether it was something he said to one of his aides or presented in a national speech. If he said he would do something, he did it. In his 1980 campaign for presidency, one promise that he gave was that, if elected, he would appoint a qualified woman to the Supreme Court—something that had never happened in the nation's history.

On July 1, 1981, Sandra Day O'Connor met with Ronald Reagan in the Oval Office of the White House. They talked for 45 minutes, and when they emerged, Reagan was clear on the matter—he didn't need to interview any other candidates to replace the retiring Supreme Court Justice Potter Stewart. He had already found the right person, and she was Sandra Day O'Connor.

Reagan appoints the first woman—Sandra Day O'Connor—to the U.S. Supreme Court. Chief Justice Warren Burger is in the center.

Sandra was born in 1930 and spent her early years riding horses and roping cattle on her parents' 155,000-acre ranch in Arizona. She graduated from high school at 16 and attended Stanford University, majoring in economics. Next came law school, graduation, and marriage to fellow student John Jay O'Connor.

The O'Connors lived in Frankfurt, West Germany, for three years, then returned to the United States, where her life was busy, including raising three sons. She held a number of jobs in state government, including one in the Arizona attorney general's office. In 1969, she was appointed to the Arizona Senate. In 1970, she was elected to a full term. In 1972, she became the majority leader—the first woman to ever hold that post. In the state senate she voted for the Equal Rights Amendment, favored enhanced property rights for women, and sought restoration of the death penalty.

Reagan's choice sparked some debate, not because she was a woman, but because her record on issues was a mixture of liberal and conservative positions. Despite this, Reagan went forward with his appointment. On September 25, 1981, O'Connor was made the 102nd member of the United States Supreme Court—the first woman justice.

During her years on the Supreme Court, O'Connor has voted conservatively on most issues. Feminists lost their enthusiasm for her at times, and the issue of abortion continued to create controversy. In 2001, she questioned the fairness of the death penalty in response to recent cases in which DNA testing proved convicted people to be innocent.

While not everyone agrees with the way O'Connor votes, she is widely respected for her dedication and intelligence. She is considered to be one of the most influential women in the United States.

Soon Reagan began a program of weight lifting and exercise that helped return him to full health. He maintained this exercise program for all the years of his presidency.

Having survived the assassination attempt, Reagan spent the spring and early summer getting his tax reduction program passed. Reagan faced a new challenge in August 1981. The air traffic controllers' union, the Professional Air Traffic Controllers Organization (PATCO), made what Reagan and his cabinet felt were excessive wage and benefit demands. The government countered with what it considered a generous offer: wage increases twice those of other federal employees. PATCO rejected the offer and called a strike for August 3.

On the morning of August 3, Reagan made this statement in the Rose Garden of the White House: "Let me make one thing plain. I respect the right of workers in the private sector to strike. Indeed, as president of my own union, I led the first strike ever called by that union. I guess I'm maybe the first ever to hold this office who is a lifetime member of an AFL-CIO union. But we cannot compare labor-management relations in the private sector with government. Government cannot close down the assembly line. It has to provide—without interruption—the protective services which are government's reason for being. It was in recognition of this that Congress passed a law forbidding strikes by government employees against the public safety. Let me read the solemn oath taken by each of these employees... when they accepted their jobs: 'I am not participating in any strike against the Government of the United States or any agency thereof, and I will not participate while an employee of the Government of the United States or any agency thereof.'

"It is for this reason that I must tell those who fail to report for duty this morning that they are in violation of the law, and if they do not report for work within 48 hours, they have forfeited their jobs and will be terminated."[1]

Had the leaders of PATCO paid any attention to Reagan's earlier statements about public employee strikes, they might have anticipated this action. He had long admired President Calvin Coolidge's response to the Boston police strike of 1919. Coolidge said, "There is no right to strike against the public safety by anybody, anywhere,

[1] Question-and-answer session with reporters on the Air Traffic Controllers Strike, August 3, 1981.

One of the early major issues to confront Reagan as president was the strike of 13,000 air traffic controllers. Seen here are strikers walking the picket line at the New York air route traffic control center in August 1981. Reagan stunned many people when he fired all air traffic controllers who did not return to work within 48 hours after their walkout.

at any time."[2] Alas for PATCO, its leaders underestimated President Reagan.

Some air traffic controllers returned to work; most stayed out and were terminated. Supervisory personnel took over air traffic control and kept the planes flying, albeit on reduced schedules, until new traffic controllers could be trained. Reagan's popularity soared.

At the 1983 state dinner in her honor, Queen Elizabeth's remarks kept Reagan laughing throughout the evening. A few days earlier, Queen Elizabeth and Prince Philip had joined the Reagans at their California ranch for a visit.

Throughout his public career, one of Reagan's strongest attributes was his quiet determination to pursue a few key goals. As president, he had three: straighten out the nation's economy, limit the growth and influence of the federal government, and bring the Cold War to a successful conclusion.

Neither the attempt to assassinate him nor the air traffic controllers' strike deterred him from working toward all three goals. As to the third, he knew from his intelligence briefings that the Soviet Union was devoting so much of its money to weapons production that it was seriously straining its economy. It seemed determined to get well ahead of the United States as it pursued its goal of expanding Communist influence throughout the world.

Reagan believed that in order to bring the Cold War to an end, the two sides had to begin reducing arms, especially nuclear arms. To do that, he reasoned, the United States must first rebuild its defense structure so that the Soviets could never get ahead of it. He embarked on that buildup—the Peace Through Strength program—as soon as he took office.

Although Reagan did not announce it publicly, he embarked on a strategy designed to force the Soviets to spend themselves into near-bankruptcy in an effort to keep up. Once they were on the brink of ruin, he believed, they would agree to sit down at the negotiating table and work out arms reduction agreements.

Reagan's passion for arms reduction ran counter to the "conventional wisdom" that had prevailed through several presidencies of both parties. That view supported agreements that simply slowed the rate of *growth* of strategic arms. The idea behind it was that both the United States and the Soviet Union would have such large and frightening arsenals that neither would use them because it would result in "mutually assured destruction." The arms control program went by that name, Mutually Assured Destruction—"MAD" for short. Reagan thought it was just that, *mad.* Instead, he believed arms *reduction* should be the goal.

Reagan meets with his National Security Council in the White House Cabinet Room. Seen with Reagan are National Security Adviser Richard Allen (second from left), Secretary of State Alexander Haig (next to Reagan), and an unidentified fourth man.

[2]President Coolidge made the statement in a public exchange of letters with Samuel Gompers, president of the American Federation of Labor.

In the summer of 1981, fully recovered from the assassination attempt, he spoke at the University of Notre Dame, saying that communism would one day be consigned to "the ash heap of history." In June 1982, in London he addressed both Houses of Parliament at Westminster in which he enunciated what would become known as the Reagan Doctrine. That is, that the United States would help every democratic movement within the Communist orbit with moral and practical (but not military) support until those nations were free. This was a reversal of the Brezhnev Doctrine, that once a country became Communist it would always be Communist.

Three critical events occurred in 1983. They were important because they ended the Cold War and put Communism out of business.

On March 8, Reagan addressed the National Association of Evangelicals in Orlando, Florida. In his speech, Reagan branded the Soviet Union an "evil empire." Supporters of the "MAD" approach to arms control were, so to speak, up in arms. Political and media critics scolded Reagan for what they thought was ill-considered, reckless language. Reagan knew what he was doing. He was sure that not only millions of Americans, but also people trapped behind the "Iron Curtain," knew that what he said was true.

We now know, from writings and briefings by former Soviet officials, that Reagan's speech was closely followed in the Kremlin and that its leaders were worried that he meant what he said about rebuilding U.S. defenses. He also knew that he was challenging the legitimacy of their regime.

Reagan with Chancellor Helmut Kohl of Germany.

Two weeks later, on March 23, Reagan spoke to the nation over television from the Oval Office. He announced the Strategic Defense Initiative, a program that ultimately would put a missile-defense "shield" around the United States, capable of shooting down any incoming missiles. Once developed, he said, we would offer it to others, even the Soviet Union, inasmuch as an effective missile defense would render the need for continuing arms buildup obsolete.

"MAD" supporters denounced the SDI as "unworkable" and "dangerous." Political opponents and the news media dubbed it "Star Wars." This effort to trivialize Reagan's plan had no effect on him, for his message had been aimed directly at the Kremlin, where its leaders understood its implications all too well. They could not afford to expand their conventional and nuclear arsenal and also build an SDI-equivalent without courting financial ruin.

Reagan knew that the Soviet leaders were aware that the United States had the monetary and technical resources to develop an SDI system, but they had previously thought we lacked the political will to do so. Reagan was telling them he would supply that political will.

The seeds of Reagan's SDI plan had been planted many years before. In 1967, his first year as governor of California, he visited the Lawrence Livermore Laboratory at the invitation of Dr. Edward Teller, then its director. He spent a day learning what the scientists there were working on: plans for a Strategic Defense Initiative. Then, in July 1979, he was invited to visit NORAD headquarters deep in a Colorado mountain where the armed services could monitor missile activity. The sophisticated equipment, which could detect on a moment's notice any missile launched at the United States, impressed him. In the next moment he was appalled to realize that all we could do in reponse was to launch our own missiles: Mutually Assured Destruction.

Late that summer he received a briefing from the Carter White House on the freshly negotiated Strategic Arms Limitation Treaty (SALT). Like

Reagan ordered an invasion of the Caribbean Island of Grenada in November 1983 to oust a Communist regime. Here he discusses his decision at a White House press briefing. Newly appointed Middle East Envoy Donald Rumsfeld stands to the right.

SALT I, it simply called for a limit on the rate of increase of nuclear arms. He announced his opposition to the treaty. He said what we needed were Strategic Arms *Reduction* Treaties (he got his first nearly nine years later).

Not long after his SDI speech another milestone in the effort to end the Cold War occurred. The then-young government of German Chancellor Helmut Kohl decided to deploy Pershing cruise missiles in that country. The decision was not an easy one, for it was made in the face of huge street demonstrations throughout Germany, orchestrated and egged on by Soviet agents and sympathizers. Once made, however, the decision led other Western European allies to follow with placement of cruise missiles. NATO thus checkmated the Soviet Union's intermediate-range SS-20 missiles, which had been aimed at Western European capitals for several years.

In October 1983, U.S. forces invaded the Caribbean island of Grenada, freeing it from a Communist government that had overthrown the previous government and threatened to become a launching pad for Cuban and Soviet expansion in the Western Hemisphere. Critics claimed Reagan had invaded Grenada to distract attention from the suicide truck bombing of the Marine barracks in Beirut, Lebanon, the day before. This reasoning is not possible, however, for an invasion requiring the support and secrecy employed at Grenada could not have been carried out on a day's notice.

Reagan hoped and believed these actions would lead to a summit with the Soviets in which strategic arms reduction would be discussed. Instead, as he put it, their leaders "kept dying on me." First Brezhnev, then Andropov, then Chernenko succumbed before such a meeting could be held. It was not until after Mikhail Gorbachev came to power in the spring of 1985 during Reagan's second term that a summit was scheduled. Reagan and Gorbachev met at Lake Geneva, Switzerland, in November.

At the first meeting, before a warming fire in a boat house by the lake, with only their interpreters present, Reagan said to Gorbachev, "We don't mistrust each other because we're armed. We're armed because we mistrust each other. We have two alternatives: to find a way to trust one another enough to begin to reduce arms, or to have an all-out arms race. Mr. Gorbachev, that's a race you can't win."[3] Reagan later said that

During his presidency, Reagan would often confront General Secretary Mikhail Gorbachev of the former Soviet Union, but they had a mutual respect for each other that continued even after Reagan's years in the White House.

[3] Verbal exchange provided by Peter Hannaford.

Gorbachev not only understood but also appreciated what he had just said. They discussed areas of agreement and disagreement and determined to meet again.

The next summit, October 11 and 12, 1986, in Reykjavik, Iceland, was convened hastily, at Gorbachev's request. On the first day they agreed to the rapid elimination of nuclear missiles in Europe and to the eventual elimination of all ballistic missiles—the "Zero Option"—over a period of ten years. Reagan offered to share SDI technology with the Soviet Union and to refrain from deploying the SDI unilaterally for ten years.

On the second day, Gorbachev offered major reductions in the Soviet Union's conventional forces. Reagan was elated until he learned there were conditions. "I thought we were in complete agreement," he later said to Gorbachev, who then smiled and said, "This all depends, of course, on you giving up SDI." Reagan was shocked, reminding him that he had offered to share SDI technology. Gorbachev said he did not believe the pledge. For Reagan, that was it. He said, "The meeting's over. Let's go, George [Shultz, his secretary of state], we're leaving."[4]

Reagan and Nancy did a great deal of diplomatic traveling during his presidency. They are pictured here at the Great Wall in China in April 1984.

As Reagan left, Gorbachev cried, "I don't know what else I could have done." Angrily, Reagan replied, "You could have said, 'yes.'"[5]

As it turned out, this was the climactic event in the Cold War. Realizing he could not stop Reagan from developing SDI, that his economy would not hold out much longer at his country's current pace of arms spending, he introduced *glasnost* (limited free speech) and *perestroika,* an attempt to modernize the creaky Soviet economic system. But when people with no freedom get some, they want more. Gorbachev could not stop the movement. *Perestroika* did not work. Demands increased for greater reforms; the ring of satellite states in Central and Eastern Europe demanded an end to Soviet domination. The end of the Cold War was in sight.

Reagan and Gorbachev had two more summits, in Washington in 1987 and Moscow in 1988. They signed the first arms reduction agreement to reduce intermediate missiles (the INF treaty) and began informal discussions about reducing intercontinental ballistic missiles. Taking advantage of the new openness in Soviet society, Reagan met at the U.S. Embassy in Moscow with a group of dissidents, human rights advocates, and intellectuals for a roundtable discussion and reception. He spoke to the students at Moscow University. Standing below a bust of Lenin, he said things that would not have been permitted in Moscow a few years before:

"We Americans make no secret of our belief in freedom. In fact . . . Freedom is the right to question and change the established way of doing things. It is the continuing revolution of the marketplace. It is the understanding that allows us to recognize shortcomings and seek solutions. It is the right to set forth an idea, scoffed at by experts, and watch it catch fire among the people. It is the right to dream—to follow your dream or stick to your conscience, even if you're the only one in a sea of doubters.

---

[4] Verbal exchange provided by Peter Hannaford.

[5] See chapter 1 of *Recollections of Reagan* by Peter Hannaford.

Reagan escorts his daughter Patti at her wedding in August 1984 to Paul Grilley. Although father and daughter had their differences, Patti asked her dad to give her away at the ceremony.

"Freedom is the recognition that no single person, no single authority or government has a monopoly on the truth, but that every individual life is infinitely precious, that every one of us put on this earth has been put there for a reason and has something to offer."[6]

Soon after the Moscow summit, the Soviet Union began its withdrawal from Afghanistan, which it had invaded nine years earlier.

Problems in the Middle East had also challenged Reagan throughout his presidency, but one event during his first term especially troubled him deeply. In 1982, Israel had invaded Lebanon. This prompted Reagan to send the Marines into Beirut (as part of a multinational force) to see that the PLO was evacuated from the country. In the course of the Israeli invasion, massacres had occurred in some Palestinian refugee camps by members of a Lebanese militia.

A year later, on the morning of October 23, 1983, a truck driven by a Shiite Muslim on a suicide mission crashed into the U.S. Marines' compound near the Beirut International Airport. Twelve thousand pounds of TNT killed 234 American soldiers from the First Battalion, 8th Marine Regiment. Another 112 were pulled out of the devastation. Many of them were permanently injured. The blast created a crater 30 feet deep and 40 feet across. It was a blow to the United States, and especially to Reagan. He immediately pulled out the rest of the Marines from Lebanon. The tragedy was written on Reagan's face at the memorial service.

Another event occurred nearly a year later. Though it was not significant to the nation, it was to the Reagans. On August 14, 1984, Reagan's daughter Patti married Paul Grilley, and despite the estranged relationship between parents and daughter, Reagan escorted his daughter down the aisle. This was unusual because they had not attended the wedding of their son, Ron, in 1980 or that of their other daughter, Maureen, in 1981. As close as he was to the American people and to Nancy, he had not developed the same intimacy with his children. Only after he retired from the presidency and his health problems became apparent would the longtime rift between parents and children finally heal.

As Reagan's first term came to an end, the nation was feeling far more positive than it had earlier. The economy was moving forward, as he had promised. Unemployment and inflation were down and continuing to decline. Manufacturing was up—making U.S. products more competitive in world trade. He had kept virtually all of his campaign promises, from boosting national defense and cutting taxes to slowing the flood of Japanese cars into the American market and lifting the grain embargo against the USSR. Reagan's popularity was at an all-time high, and he knew that even though Nancy might hope he would be a one-term president, it wasn't time to quit—not yet.

---

[6]President Reagan's speech at Moscow State University, USSR, on May 31, 1988.

Chapter Eight

A Term of Highs and Lows

The Great Communicator faces Gorbachev, the loss of Challenger, Iran-Contra, and cancer—all in one term.

It came as no surprise when Reagan announced that he would run for president again in 1984. This time, the theme of his election was "Morning in America." He had achieved two of his main goals during his first term: the passage of a 25 percent across-the-board tax cut and restoration of the nation's defenses. His new campaign focused on optimism, hope, and patriotism—qualities that Reagan knew how to project and share with the nation's voters. It was a successful campaign and a decidedly more confident one than that of his Democratic opponent, Walter Mondale.

Reagan's campaign got off to a rocky start, however. In his first debate with Mondale on October 7 in Louisville, Kentucky, he was somewhat off track. Nancy agonized for him from the sidelines. Mondale had come from the campaign trail and was prepared, having recently debated candidates in the Democratic primaries. Mondale was respectful toward Reagan, but it was the kind of respect a person gives to his elderly relatives, not a fellow politician. When Mondale used Reagan's old line of "There you go again" regarding Medicare, Reagan became confused and upset, and his uncertainty was obvious to the audience and to the camera. Even Reagan felt he had done poorly, blaming it primarily on over-preparation. He was embarrassed at his less than stellar performance and was determined to do better the second time.

Nancy knew her husband's confidence had been shaken and realized if he was going to do well in the next debate, he needed that confidence back. She arranged for Stuart Spencer, Reagan's political consultant from his gubernato-

After the harsh reactions and jeering he received from students during his campaigns for governor in the late 1960s and early 1970s, Reagan was pleased to be so strongly welcomed by youth during his second presidential campaign.

rial campaigns, as well as Senator Paul Laxalt, to spend some time alone with Reagan. They were there to give him a pep talk and convince him that he could certainly win the second debate. Media consultant Roger Ailes was also brought in to counsel Reagan, and a long letter of support arrived from friend Richard Nixon.

Nancy stands in the center while Chief Justice Warren E. Burger swears Reagan in for his second presidential term.

The second debate over foreign affairs on October 21 in Kansas City made up for the first one, as Reagan was sharp, witty, and completely prepared. At an age most men are settled into retirement and slowing down, Reagan was facing another four years as head of the country. In fact, during the debates, when he was asked if he had any doubts about being able to function during a crisis at his advanced age, he charmed people with his quick response. "Not at all," he replied. "And I want you to know that also I will not make age an issue in this campaign. I am not going to exploit for political purposes my opponent's youth and inexperience."[1] Even Mondale had to laugh at that witty line. Once again, Americans had confidence in Reagan's abilities, and talk of his advanced age faded into the background.

Reagan committed what the media seized on as a "gaffe" in late summer. When he was preparing for his weekly radio address, which was to be broadcast from his ranch, he did not realize that the microphone was already turned on when he made a quip during what he thought was a microphone check of his voice level. He joked about "outlawing" Russia and getting ready to bomb in a few minutes. Over the years he had often used irreverent jests as "mike" tests; however, there were momentary worries that he might have been serious this time. Ultimately, it was accepted for what it was—a quip never intended for the public's ears.

In the subsequent weeks, Reagan would more than make up for this slip. He and Nancy put in an appearance at the summer Olympic Games in Los Angeles, and on June 6, they participated in a commemoration of the D-Day landings in 1944. Reagan gave an inspiring speech at Pointe du Hoc to a group of U.S. Rangers who, back in 1944, had actually scaled the cliffs behind him as part of the liberation of Europe from the Nazis. Reagan's words struck the hearts of these men who had put their lives on the line for their country decades ago. "These are the boys of Pointe du Hoc. These are the men who took the cliffs," he said. "These are the champions who helped free a continent. These are the heroes who helped end a war."[2] His intense and uplifting words brought tears to the Rangers' eyes, as well as to those of the reporters and Secret Service agents. These words also made him even more popular than he had been before and cemented his image as "The Great Communicator."

Following his speech, Reagan and his wife knelt in prayer at the Omaha Beach chapel and took a tour of the Normandy American cemetery. It was a sobering sight. More than nine thousand simple white crosses and Stars of David were spread out across the ground in a field of sorrow. Before the day was over, Reagan gave another speech and read from a letter written by an Army veteran who had been in D-Day's first assault and lived. That day, his daughter was there to put

[1] Quote is from one of the 1984 presidential debates between Reagan and Mondale.

[2] Quote is from a June 6, 1984, speech commemorating the D-Day landings and given in Normandy, France.

flowers on the graves of his fallen brothers. It was a poignant moment for everyone.

Reagan's reelection victory would be the biggest one in presidential history: a landslide of 525 electoral votes to Mondale's 10, and it would usher in four years of peace and prosperity for the entire nation. No longer was there a need to ask the American people if they were better off now than they had been four years ago. The answer to that was obvious.

The day after Mondale called to concede, Reagan and Nancy headed back to their ranch for three days. While the ranch was where Reagan restored his energy and vigor, it certainly wasn't because he spent his time there lying around. If he wasn't on the back of a horse, he was splitting wood, clearing brush, and building or mending fences. Photos of the president in his jeans and flannel shirts, saw in hand, again made him seem familiar and likable to people far and wide.

An analysis of those who voted for Reagan in the reelection gives testimony to his uncanny ability to touch and charm a wide range of people. Six out of every ten independents had cast their votes for Reagan; even more surprisingly, one in four registered Democrats did as well. While most of the Jewish and African American voters cast their ballots for Mondale, Reagan won the majority of Protestants and Catholics. Perhaps most surprising of all was that he also won 60 percent of the youngest voters (ages 18 to 24)—a record for a Republican candidate.

Although he entered his second term with energy and passion, the next four years would bring both high and low points in his public career. The term would cement his image with the American people as a strong leader with a devout dedication to his country's safety and confidence in its future, but there would be some pitfalls along the way.

As we have seen, Reagan's four summits with Mikhail Gorbachev led to the solid beginning of the strategic arms reduction process. Reagan had achieved exactly what he had hoped to, and the peace between the two countries may well be his greatest legacy as president. After Reagan's presidency, the two men would maintain their friendship and would visit each other on several occasions.

The first controversy of Reagan's second term didn't take long to pop up. In 1985 German Chancellor Helmut Kohl asked Reagan to visit a German cemetery in honor of the 40th anniversary of the end of World War II. It would be a good opportunity to show the unity between the two countries.

After Reagan's scheduled visit to Bitburg Cemetery was announced, an unexpected discovery put an entirely new light on the matter. It was revealed that 50 of the 2,000 German soldiers buried in the cemetery were actually members of Hitler's elite SS. Jewish organizations were outraged that Reagan would consider such a visit. His staff advised him to cancel the appearance, but he refused. Instead, before he went to Bitburg, he and Nancy spent time at the Bergen-Belsen

Controversy surrounded Reagan's visit to Bitburg Cemetery in Germany during his second term. Because Nazi S.S. soldiers were buried there, his trip was seen as a potential public relations disaster. Reagan's visit to the Bergen-Belsen concentration camp, where he paid homage to the Jews who had lost their lives in the war, mitigated the criticism.

A somber moment for President and Mrs. Reagan while they attend the memorial services for the crew of the Challenger space shuttle on January 28, 1986. Reagan's words of comfort and reassurance were aired once again in early 2003 when another space shuttle crew was lost.

concentration camp, looking at pictures and other artifacts from the Holocaust. It was a sobering experience for both of them, and it helped counterbalance the stop at Bitburg.

In early 1986, another event would force Reagan to demonstrate his presidential skills when the entire country shared in the shock and horror of the Challenger explosion. The nation had become rather complacent about the space program, taking for granted the technology that went into these space shuttle flights and forgetting the inherent risk in each mission. The Challenger's mission was the first to include a civilian, a mother and teacher named Christa McAuliffe. That fact seemed to make the tragedy even more difficult to accept.

The day of the explosion, Reagan was scheduled to give his annual State of the Union speech. Instead, he spoke to the nation about the Challenger disaster and how, despite the day's sorrow, the space program should and would continue. As usual, his words of hope comforted the nation. That was one of Reagan's most enduring and endearing traits. "The crew of the space shuttle Challenger honored us by the manner in which they lived their lives," he said. "We will never forget them, nor the last time we saw them, this morning, as they prepared for the journey and waved goodbye and 'slipped the surly bonds of Earth to touch the face of God.'"[3]

Reagan also struggled several times during his term about what to do about terrorism. Although he abhorred it, he also hesitated to react to it with military action because of the inevitable risk to civilians. In April 1986, he believed he had no choice. A West Berlin disco had been bombed, and 200 people were injured, including 63 American soldiers. A U.S. serviceman and civilian died in the blast. Intelligence agencies had obtained evidence that determined that Libyans did the bombing. Reagan knew a message needed to be sent. Therefore, he ordered U.S. Air Force and Navy bombers based in England to attack the Libyan cities of Tripoli and Benghazi. The air strike was dubbed Operation El Dorado Canyon. The size of the strike was large, with approximately one hundred aircraft launched to accomplish the mission. Reagan timed the strike to occur just as he went on national television to explain to the American people why he had ordered the attack—that it was an act of self-defense, which was the country's right and duty.

The planes dropped ninety 2,000-pound bombs. At least two of those hit the residence of

The President and First Lady had the opportunity to meet many famous people during his two terms in the White House. Here, they speak with Prince Charles and Princess Diana.

[3]Bill Adler, *The Uncommon Wisdom of Ronald Reagan*, 88.

Libyan leader Moammar Qaddafi. Instead of hurting him, however, the bombs killed his daughter and wounded two of his sons, along with many other civilians. Qaddafi himself escaped without a scratch since he had been sleeping in a nearby tent. The majority of Americans applauded Reagan's decision, and following his speech, the White House received more than 286,000 calls in response, three-quarters of which were favorable. Operation El Dorado Canyon was a success, for Qaddafi's terrorists were silenced.

During the course of the second term, one of the biggest issues that Reagan had to deal with was a personal one—his health and Nancy's. It was often difficult to remember while watching this dynamic couple that he was in his 70s, she in her late 60s—ages when many human bodies begin to slow down and develop problems. Both were diagnosed with cancer. In 1985, a mass was found in his colon, and surgery verified that it was malignant. Fortunately, the disease had not spread, and after losing about two feet of intestines, Reagan was able to return home. As he was recovering, however, his physicians discovered a patch of skin cancer on his nose and removed it. Two years later, the spot would return and, once again, would be surgically removed. In 1987, Reagan would undergo surgery once more, this time for prostate cancer. As if these physical ailments weren't enough, another trial was around the corner.

During the course of a regular mammogram, a tumor was found in Nancy's left breast, and it was malignant. She had chosen to have a mastectomy, rather than a lumpectomy, with its necessary follow-up chemotherapy. She wanted to have the whole ordeal over with quickly because she knew that neither she nor he would be able to keep up their duties if she was dealing with the effects of chemotherapy. Reagan felt despair and frustration as Nancy underwent surgery. He had truly believed that nothing could ever happen to her; she was his support and his guiding force in the world. As their daughter, Patti, once said, they completed each other. He stayed right by her side before and after the surgery, and their dedication to each other was obvious to anyone who saw them.

A matter of days after Nancy's surgery, while she was still bedridden, she was hit with another

Reagan and the First Lady look at the flowers sent to Nancy following her breast surgery in 1987. Compounded by the death of her mother, this was a stressful time for Nancy, and she deeply appreciated this showing of kindness and concern by well-wishers.

I LOVE YOU, RONNIE

In 2000, Nancy Reagan and Random House published a book called *I Love You, Ronnie*. In it were the letters, cards, and notes that Reagan had written to his wife over the years. It gave an intimate, personal look at the marriage, which people had watched for decades. It also is further proof of what a romantic Reagan was.

Nancy wasn't sure what to do with all of these letters. She didn't want them lost or to run the risk of someone finding them and selling them, so she put them into a book. The proceeds for the sales are split between the National Alzheimer's Association and Ronald Reagan Presidential Foundation.

An example of one of Reagan's letters to his beloved wife reads:

Dear First Lady,

As president of the United States, it's my honor and privilege to cite you for service above and beyond the call of duty in that you have made one man, me, the most happy man in the world for 29 years.

Beginning in 1951, Nancy Davis sealed the plight of a lonely man who didn't know how lonely he really was, determined to rescue him from a completely empty life, refusing to be rebuffed by a certain amount of stupidity on his part. She ignored his somewhat slow response. With patience and tenderness, she gradually brought the light of understanding to his darkened, obtuse mind, and he discovered the joy of loving someone with all his heart.

Nancy Davis then went on to bring him happiness for the next 29 years as Nancy Davis Reagan, for which she received and will continue to receive his undying devotion forever and ever. She has done this in spite of the fact that he still can't find the words to tell her how lost he would be without her. He sits in the Oval Office from which he can see, if he scrunches down, her window and feels warm all over just knowing she is there. The above is the statement of the man who benefited from her act of heroism. The below is his signature.

Ronald Reagan, President of the United States.

P.S. He, I mean, I, love and adore you.[4]

blow—the death of her mother, Edith, or Deede as the family called her. Nancy and her mother had been close all of their lives, talking almost daily. Her mother's death was very hard on Nancy, especially since it came right after her operation. The funeral was difficult for her, and it was made more so when Patti refused to attend. Reagan agonized over the fact that even though he was in a position of tremendous power, he couldn't do anything to help his wife through this traumatic time. All he could do was love her, hold her, and pray for her.

The Reagans went public with their ailments to encourage other Americans to appreciate the value of early medical detection and prompt treatment. They felt that by coming forward about their own conditions they could help others to seek help. They would do the same years down the road when Reagan was diagnosed with Alzheimer's disease.

While the highest point of his presidency was his work to end the Cold War, Reagan's low point

[4]See *I Love You, Ronnie* by Nancy Reagan and Ronald Reagan.

was one that would cause his approval rating to drop by a half. It would not only make Reagan doubt himself but would also make the nation wonder if perhaps age was finally catching up with him. It would even bring about rumors of impeachment.

In November 1986, a story appeared in a Beirut magazine asserting that the United States was selling arms to Iran. Supposedly, they were doing this in return for Iran's help in getting five American hostages released from Muslim terrorists in Lebanon. The U.S. press picked up the story. They researched and investigated, and they discovered that the story was true. This covert activity violated Reagan's promise that he would never make deals or negotiate in any way with terrorist governments or their sponsors, let alone one controlled by the Ayatollah Khomeini.

Before the White House could react to the story, another detail came to light that complicated matters and made the picture seem even worse. Not only had the United States arranged to give the Iranians 3,300 antitank missiles and 50 HAWK antiaircraft missiles, the profit from the deal had been channeled to the Contras, the guerrillas fighting the pro-Communist Sandinista regime in Nicaragua. There was confusion as to whether this was legal. Many Democrats in Congress argued that it violated a Congressional ban on helping the Contras. Defenders of the administration took the position that these particular transactions were outside the scope of the Congressional ban. Nevertheless, there was widespread public dismay and criticism of Reagan and his administration.

Reagan swore that he had no personal knowledge of either of these actions. Instead, the blame fell largely on two people—John Poindexter, the National Security Adviser, and Oliver North, a Marine colonel. Reagan was convinced that they had agreed to these procedures without telling him anything about them and was appalled that these deals had been made. Poindexter resigned immediately, and North was subsequently fired. Both men would later be found guilty in a federal trial, but their convictions would be overturned.

Lieutenant Colonel Oliver North was one of the primary people involved in the Iran-Contra issue. North later ran for U.S. senator in Virginia in 1994, but he lost.

Without hesitation, Reagan did what he needed to do. On March 19, 1987, in a televised address from the East Room of the White House, he faced a rather hostile press and told his side of the story to the American people. Though he had often expressed a desire to free the hostages, he had not been aware that his staff had sold weapons to the Iranians, nor that the profits from the arrangement had gone to the Contras. He immediately endorsed three separate investigations into what was by now called the Iran-Contra affair, including one by independent prosecutor Lawrence Walsh. Walsh's study concluded that no evidence proved Reagan ever knew about the weapons exchange or the funneling of funds. In a later speech, Reagan told the voters that "A few months ago, I told the American people that I did not trade arms for hostages. My heart and my best intentions still tell me that's true but the facts and the evidence tell me it's not."[5] Reagan weathered this storm and came out of it scarred but without any permanent damage. In fact, his approval rating quickly rebounded to previous heights.

In 1985, Reagan tackled a growing issue—AIDS. His administration had told him to stay away from the topic because of the controversy associated with it. Thus far, he had listened. Soon after Rock Hudson died of AIDS, however, Reagan told the Health and Human Services department that the fight against the disease should be a major public health priority.

When Reagan left the presidency, he had the highest approval rating of any president up to that time. He was loved by some and respected by many. One of the stories that a former Reagan speechwriter, Peggy Noonan, tells shows the warm, personal side of this unique president. It concerns an 83-year-old woman named Frances Green, who lived outside of San Francisco. She didn't have much money, but for eight years, she had made certain to send one dollar each year to the Republican National Convention.

One day, in Frances's mail, there was an invitation from the party asking her, as a donor, to come to the White House to meet President Reagan. She overlooked the RSVP, though, which mentioned that a positive response was required and should be accompanied by a generous donation. She thought she was invited because of their appreciation for her annual one-dollar donation.

Frances put together all the money she possibly could and climbed aboard a train for the four-day trip to Washington. She arrived at the White House, complete with her white hair, white stockings, white dress, and hat with white netting. Despite her enthusiasm, she was turned away at the gate because her name was nowhere on the guest list. Frances was devastated. Fortunately, a Ford Motor Company executive standing behind her heard the whole story and asked her to return the following morning to meet him.

[5] Adler, 99.

Actor Rock Hudson, one of the many victims of AIDS, was a friend of the Reagans. His tragic death helped persuade Reagan to allocate more money and effort into eradicating the disease.

She agreed, and the executive immediately made contact with a presidential aide to get her cleared for a tour the next day.

Frances returned in the morning, and as promised, the Ford executive gave her a lovely tour. In other parts of the White House, however, things were far from calm. Ed Meese had just resigned; global troubles needed attention; and Reagan was spending the day in and out of important conferences and top-secret meetings. The Ford executive had hoped that Frances might get a quick glimpse of Reagan moving from one room to the next, if she were lucky.

People were coming and going in all directions, and suddenly, Reagan, who had been told about Frances's visit the day before, spotted the elderly lady in the hallway. He motioned for her to come into his office, and with characteristic kindness, acted as if the computers had made a mistake and not let him know she had arrived,

An Excerpt from the Speech Made at Brandenburg Gate, Berlin, June 12, 1987

The speech that Reagan made at the Brandenburg Gate shows the power and gripping emotion that he could put into his speeches. Here are several excerpts:

"We welcome change and openness; for we believe that freedom and security go together, that the advance of human liberty can only strengthen the cause of world peace. There is one sign the Soviets can make that would be unmistakable, that would advance dramatically the cause of freedom and peace.

General Secretary Gorbachev, if you seek peace, if you seek prosperity for the Soviet Union and Eastern Europe, if you seek liberalization: Come here to this gate! Mr. Gorbachev, open this gate! Mr. Gorbachev, tear down this wall!

... Today thus represents a moment of hope. We in the West stand ready to cooperate with the East to promote true openness, to break down barriers that separate people, to create a safe, freer world. And surely there is no better place than Berlin, the meeting place of West and East, to make a start.

... As I looked out a moment ago from the Reichstag, that embodiment of German unity, I noticed words crudely spray-painted upon the wall, perhaps by a young Berliner: 'This wall will fall. Beliefs become reality.' Yes, across Europe, this wall will fall. For it cannot withstand faith; it cannot withstand truth. The wall cannot withstand freedom."

Reagan's words at the Brandenburg Gate echoed out across an audience of tens of thousands of West Berliners. Unseen are the thousands of East Berliners who were listening from the other side of the wall, despite the efforts of police to stop them.

Reagan's parting address to the nation at the end of his two terms once more reminded people why he had been called "The Great Communicator." As usual, his words were inspiring and confident of a strong future for the country.

otherwise he would have gone out to the front to greet her himself. He asked her to sit down, and for the next 20 minutes, they talked about her family and hometown. It was an amazing moment for Frances Green. While some might say that his time—valuable time—was wasted that day, many others would smile and say that gesture of kindness is what made Reagan the beloved president—and man—that he was.

Reagan's final address to the American people as president of the United States was on January 11, 1989. As usual, he gave most of the credit to others. "My friends, we did it," he said. "We weren't just marking time. We made a difference. We made the country stronger. We made the country freer and we left her in good hands. All in all, not bad, not bad at all."[6]

The now former president and First Lady wave a heartfelt farewell to well-wishers who came by to express their respect for the retiring couple as they left for the trip home to California.

[6] Adler, 113.

CHAPTER NINE

THE SUNSET OF LIFE

A new phase in life is cut short by Alzheimer's—and a beloved president is remembered and honored.

Ronald Reagan left the White House with the highest approval rating of any U.S. president—63 percent. As sorry as he was to go, the American people were also saddened to say good-bye. Many looked at him as a fatherly figure who loved his country and its people. Reagan achieved many of his goals as president, especially restoring the nation's economic strength and moving the Cold War toward its conclusion.

He had hoped to bring about comprehensive welfare reform during his terms. This reform did not occur until 1995, after he had left office, although it is certainly part of his legacy. He also regretted that he had been unable to achieve a balanced budget amendment to the U.S. Constitution.

Both Reagan and Nancy looked forward to their years of retirement together. They found renewal, comfort, and happiness at their California ranch—and, as always, with each other.

When the Reagans left the White House for the last time, they did so with both sadness and pleasure. They had loved their years in Washington, but now they were looking forward to a quiet retirement at their ranch in California. After eight years of being in the public eye as the leader of the most powerful nation, he was ready to relax and get back to leading a relatively normal life, and so was Nancy.

Despite the fact that Reagan was approaching 80, he wasn't one to stay still for long. He and Nancy were invited to an endless stream of banquets and ceremonies. Now that he had the time, Reagan did more writing than ever. In addition to several newspaper and magazine articles, he also wrote his second autobiography, *An American Life*.

Reagan was honored in many ways after his retirement. For example, he received the American Liberties Medallion at the American Jewish Committee's 83rd Annual National Executive Council Dinner in Beverly Hills, California. The award was in appreciation for the close ties he and his administration had kept with the Jewish community.

Reagan was also much in demand as a speaker by organizations throughout the world. In 1989, he flew to Japan for a series of speeches. Traveling and speaking to people across the globe reminded him of his days with General Electric. He and Nancy did other traveling

After leaving the White House, Reagan worked on his second autobiography, entitled An American Life. *Published in 1990, the 700-page book provided a personal, inside look at how Reagan felt about his background, his years in Hollywood and in politics, and the hope he held for the country in the years to come.*

including trips to England, Germany, Poland, and Russia. He gave reflective speeches at most of these stops and was greeted warmly—indeed, as a hero—wherever they went.

During the first year of Reagan's retirement, he had a horseback riding accident on a friend's ranch in Mexico and suffered a concussion. A couple of months later, he had minor surgery to drain some excess blood from the surface of his brain. A portion of his head had to be shaved for the operation, and he showed it off to reporters, much to the dismay of his wife. His recovery from the surgery was slow, but that was to be expected in a man of his age. Other than that, Reagan's health appeared to be excellent.

The Reagans' social life continued at a less hectic pace than in the White House days, but it was still filled with many events. In January 1990, while standing next to another legend—Mickey Mouse—Reagan rode in Disneyland's Main Street Parade to celebrate the 35th anniversary of the famous theme park. He and Nancy also made appearances at the annual Nancy Reagan Tennis Tournament held in Los Angeles. The proceeds from the games went to the Nancy Reagan Foundation, an organization that provided financial help to associations that battle drug abuse.

That same year the Berlin Wall came down. It marked the fulfillment of Reagan's words at the Brandenburg Gate, where he called for the gate to be opened and the wall to be torn down—a wall that had marked the division between East and West. Germany was finally unified once more, and Reagan's work had helped this happen. In September, the Reagans traveled to Germany so they could witness firsthand the fallen Berlin Wall. (A segment of the Wall stands today outside the Reagan Library.)

Reagan also spent a great deal of time in the fall of 1990 making speeches and videos for Republican candidates throughout the country. He even took a nostalgic trip back to Dixon, Illinois, visiting his old home and posing with the Dixon High football team.

One of Reagan's biggest projects, completed in 1991, was the building of the Ronald Reagan Presidential Library and Museum in Simi Valley, California. Built with private funds raised by the

Reagan waves hello from Disneyland, where he helped celebrate the theme park's 35th anniversary in January 1990. Pictured with him, left to right, are Minnie Mouse, Roy Disney, Michael Eisner, Art Linkletter, Bob Cummings, and, of course, Mickey Mouse.

In a rare moment in history, five U.S. presidents gather at one place for the dedication of the new Ronald Reagan Presidential Library. Pictured from left to right are George Bush, Ronald Reagan, Jimmy Carter, Gerald Ford, and Richard Nixon.

Ronald Reagan Presidential Foundation, this 153,000-square-foot building is dedicated to the four basic principles that Reagan stood for: individual liberty, economic opportunity, global democracy, and national pride. This Spanish-style building sits on a 100-acre tract and has four different levels. The two floors above ground contain the museum, the museum store, and various offices. The two floors below ground provide storage for the more than 100,000 gifts given to the Reagans during his presidency. They are also home to more than 55 million pages of government records, 1.5 million photographs, and 769,000 feet of movie film.

The dedication ceremony for the museum was an especially unique occasion. Gathered together in one place to honor the new building were former Presidents Richard Nixon, Gerald Ford, and Jimmy Carter—as well as Reagan and President George Bush, Sr.—with their wives. Lady Bird Johnson, Lyndon Johnson's widow, was also there.

In May 1992, the Reagans played host to Mikhail and Raisa Gorbachev at Rancho del Cielo before bestowing the first Ronald Reagan Presidential Freedom Award on Gorbachev. (Reagan gave Gorbachev a tour of the ranch, by Jeep.)

The Gorbachevs came to visit the Reagans in May 1992 and seemed surprised that the Reagans lived on such a modest ranch.

At the August 1992 Republican National Convention, Reagan urged people to vote for incumbent President George Bush, Sr. Echoing the theme of his earlier speeches, he stated that it was once more a time for choosing. This farewell speech to the party is considered to be one of the best of his entire political career.

The same year, Reagan wowed the audience at the Republican National Convention in Houston by giving an inspiring speech that encouraged people to vote for his successor, George Bush, Sr. Many who were present at the convention felt it was one of his best speeches ever. When the delegates shouted "four more years" at him, he responded with characteristic humor, stating that since the constitution wouldn't allow for a third term, they must all be yelling because they hoped he would be alive for four more years. The crowd loved him; not bad for a man of 81. Just a few months later, President Bush would give Reagan the Presidential Medal of Honor. He was the only president to receive this award in his lifetime.

Reagan's 81st birthday in 1992 was a gala event. The black-tie dinner in Beverly Hills raised money for the new library and museum. More than 900 guests heard keynote speaker and longtime Reagan friend, Britain's Margaret Thatcher, the former prime minister. She praised Reagan's actions, which had brought about the end of the Cold War, and applauded his enduring ability to use words to uplift and inspire people all over the world. At the gathering, Reagan made a special birthday wish, asking that God watch over all the men and women then serving in the Persian Gulf. Reagan wanted them to know that as a nation, everyone was firmly behind them.

Early in 1994 was a turning point for the Reagans. Unfortunately, it was a turn for the worse. At his 83rd birthday celebration, Reagan introduced his friend Margaret Thatcher and then toasted her. Before the crowd could applaud, his eyes returned to the top of his note cards

Great Britain's Prime Minister, Margaret Thatcher, sometimes referred to as the Iron Lady, developed a strong friendship with Reagan during his presidency. She praised his work to end the Cold War, and at his birthday gala in 1994, stated, "Not since Lincoln, or Winston Churchill in Britain, has there been a President who has so understood the power of words to uplift and inspire."

WHERE ARE THEY NOW?

Although relations were quite strained at times between the Reagans and their four children, in recent years they have come back together, reunited in a mutual love for Ronald Reagan. Each seems to have followed in his footsteps, whether it be in politics, acting, or radio.

The Reagans with Maureen and Ron and their spouses.

Maureen Reagan, his first child, died of cancer in 2001 at the age of 60. Before she passed away, she was the Honorary Chairwoman and Spokesperson for the National Alzheimer's Association. In 2000, she received the Alzheimer's Association Distinguished Service Award. She shared her father's passion for politics, and in 1982, ran in the California primaries for U.S. Senate. Reagan did not feel he could endorse her for fear of nepotism. She lost the race. Like her siblings, she wrote an autobiography, *First Father, First Daughter: A Memoir.* Although Maureen and her father disagreed on some issues, she was a longtime supporter of many of his actions.

Michael Reagan had a stormy relationship with his father for several years. When he used his dad's name in an attempt to increase his business, a four-year rift began. He wrote an autobiography, *Michael Reagan: On the Outside Looking In*, which portrayed his mother, Jane Wyman, harshly. In 1984, Reagan and his eldest son worked to repair their relationship. Since then, Michael has become a syndicated radio broadcaster. He has his own radio show that centers on politics, and each week more than two million listeners tune in to hear him and his guests.

Patti Davis, who kept her mother's maiden name, had many disagreements with her parents. Her political views often differed from theirs, and her lifestyle often upset the Reagans, including the time she posed nude with a naked man for *Playboy*. She also tried her hand at acting, appearing in several movies and television series. In her novel *Home Front*, Davis wrote of a fictional president and his wife, a thinly veiled and negative portrayal of her parents. In recent years, Patti has written a number of articles for well-known national magazines and has been the keynote speaker at conferences on Alzheimer's.

Ron Reagan, Jr., started out as a dancer with the Joffrey Ballet Company. Then he wrote for a number of publications and appeared on several television shows. In 1992, he hosted and co-produced six one-hour documentaries for E! Television and continues in a television career.

and he read the entire introduction and toast one more time. Even though the audience accepted it without comment, it was clear that something was wrong.

As far back as the days of his first presidential campaign, Reagan had asked his personal physicians to watch for any potential signs of the same mind-crippling disease that had killed his mother, Nelle, in 1962. Back then it had been called senility, but by the 1990s, it had acquired a new name: Alzheimer's. While president, he said if they ever found any indication that he had the same condition, he would immediately resign.

Despite his requested vigilance, by 1993 there was little doubt that something was going wrong with Reagan's memory. The first public acknowledgment of it came from his daughter, Maureen. One evening, while Maureen was having dinner with her father and Nancy, she told familiar World War II stories that she had heard from him years ago. When she was a girl, he had related many of the plots of the war movies he had played in. This time, however, he looked at his daughter with a blank stare and told her he had no memory of acting in the films to which she was referring. At that moment, Maureen reported a quiet click of awareness that something was wrong beyond the typical memory problems that can come with age.

Reagan and Nancy and their family show a picture of her mother.

In 1994, Reagan had a physical examination at the Mayo Clinic. It confirmed Maureen's fears and brought Reagan and Nancy—who had weathered many tragedies and trials—the toughest news they would ever have to deal with. Reagan was diagnosed with Alzheimer's disease, which came as a painful shock to this vibrant man and his wife. Nancy was crushed by the fact that after all they had weathered together—the cancers, the assassination attempt, and the stressful years in office—the worst was yet to come. They both knew that the future years would be difficult for them, and indeed they have been. In time, Nancy made sure only a few select visitors were allowed to their home. She wanted the country and its people to remember Reagan as he had been, at the peak of his powers. He made his last trip to his personal haven, Rancho del Cielo, in 1995. Two-and-a-half years later, Nancy would sell the ranch to the Young America's Foundation, a nonprofit group that would use the property to help teach college students about Reagan's life and times. They have maintained the ranch just as it was when the Reagans were there.

In April 1996, two visitors to see Reagan were Rear Admiral Robert Nutwell and Newport News Shipbuilding president William Fricks. They presented him with a model of the nuclear aircraft carrier U.S.S. *Reagan*, then under construction. In July, Republican presidential candidate Bob Dole and his wife, Elizabeth, paid the former president a brief visit. During these visits, Reagan rarely let go of Nancy's hand.

In one of the rare photos of Reagan after his announcement of Alzheimer's, he and Nancy are shown in April 1996, accepting a model of the U.S.S. Ronald Reagan *from Newport News Shipbuilding President William Fricks. Rear Admiral Robert Nutwell is also present.*

In keeping with the dignity and courage that characterized Reagan all of his life, he composed a handwritten letter to the people of the United States to share the news about the Alzheimer's diagnosis.

Nov. 5, 1994

My Fellow Americans,

I have recently been told that I am one of the millions of Americans who will be afflicted with Alzheimer's Disease.

Upon learning this news, Nancy and I had to decide whether as private citizens we would keep this a private matter or whether we would make this news known in a public way.

In the past Nancy suffered from breast cancer and I had my cancer surgeries. We found through our open disclosure we were able to raise public awareness. We were happy that as a result many more people underwent testing. They were treated in early stages and able to return to normal, healthy lives.

So now, we feel it is important to share it with you. In opening our hearts, we hope this might promote greater awareness of this condition. Perhaps it will encourage a clearer understanding of the individuals and families who are affected by it.

At the moment I feel just fine. I intend to live the remainder of the years God gives me on this earth doing the things I have always done. I will continue to share life's journey with my beloved Nancy and my family. I plan to enjoy the great outdoors and stay in touch with my friends and supporters.

Unfortunately, as Alzheimer's Disease progresses, the family often bears a heavy burden. I only wish there was some way I could spare Nancy from this painful experience. When the time comes I am confident that with your help she will face it with faith and courage.

In closing let me thank you, the American people, for giving me the great honor of allowing me to serve as your President. When the Lord calls me home whenever that may be, I will leave with the greatest love for this country of ours and eternal optimism for its future.

I now begin the journey that will lead me into the sunset of my life. I know that for America there will always be a bright dawn ahead.

Thank you my friends. May God bless you.

Sincerely,
Ronald Reagan

ABOARD THE U.S.S. *RONALD REAGAN*

Ronald Reagan was the first living president to have a United States warship named after him. The reasons behind that are clear. Because he had long supported the U.S. military, the military returned the favor by honoring him in this way.

The U.S.S. *Ronald Reagan* is an impressive ship, a Nimitz-class nuclear-powered aircraft carrier with two nuclear reactors that will not require refueling for 20 years. It is considered to be one of the most modern aircraft carriers in the world, measuring 1,092 feet long—almost as long as the Empire State Building is tall. It stretches 20 stories above the waterline, and the flight deck is more than four acres long. Construction will be completed in 2003; it is "home" to 6,000 sailors and more than 80 aircraft. It moves at speeds greater than 30 knots.

Thousands gathered at a Virginia shipyard to honor former President Reagan and the christening of the U.S.S. Ronald Reagan *on March 4, 2001. Nancy swung the traditional bottle of champagne at the bow with President Bush at her side.*

At the christening of the U.S.S. *Ronald Reagan* in March 2001, son Michael and his family were there to witness Nancy hit the side of the ship with the traditional bottle of champagne. The event was scheduled to coincide with the Reagans' 49th wedding anniversary. Lee Greenwood sang "God Bless the USA," and President George W. Bush gave a speech in which he praised Reagan's unflagging belief that the hope of universal freedom is what made this country so great. More than 6,000 people attended the event, and although an incoming storm threatened, the weather once again cooperated as it had on Reagan's first inauguration. The rain stopped for the presentation and continued when it was over. Seeing nature's cooperation, son Michael Reagan wrote in his article, "Christening the U.S.S. *Ronald Reagan*, I thought to myself, 'God has always been there for Dad.'"[1]

Also riding on the ship is a bronze profile of Reagan, centered on a piece of the original Berlin Wall, which his efforts helped bring down. Artist Chas Fagan, who created the profile, said, at the unveiling ceremony in November 2002, "The U.S.S. *Ronald Reagan* will sail with the memory of the President... The name Ronald Reagan is a bold reminder of the strength that comes from character and steadfastness."[2]

[1]Michael Reagan, "Christening the U.S.S. *Ronald Reagan*," Human Events Online, March 12, 2001.

[2]Chas Fagan, speech at the unveiling ceremony of the U.S.S. *Ronald Reagan* in November 2002.

After that letter was made public, his public appearances ended. He continued to go to his office daily for nearly three years, greeting visitors. Finally, as his memory dimmed, this practice ended, and he stayed most of the time at their Los Angeles home.

Reagan's 85th birthday in 1996 was held at Chasen's restaurant in West Hollywood. Although the restaurant had been closed for a year, it was opened in honor of the Reagans. It was at Chasen's that Nancy had gone for dinner with Reagan on their first dates, and it was there where he had proposed and where they had sat together to make their wedding plans. This $1,000-a-plate dinner raised money for the Ronald Reagan Presidential Foundation, and nearly 500 people attended, including Colin Powell, Gerald Ford, Bob Hope, and Charlton Heston. One person who did not attend was Reagan himself. A 12-foot portrait of him served as centerpiece, and Nancy raised her glass in a tearful toast to her husband, best friend, and partner for life. There wasn't a dry eye in the restaurant.

Nancy's devotion to her husband has brought her a great deal of praise in recent years. While she often responds that he would have done the same for her, there is no doubt that this care is an exhausting chore—both physically and emotionally. Her reconciliation with the children has made that burden easier to bear. Patti talks to her mother almost every day—a departure from earlier years—and Michael is a frequent visitor.

On February 6, 1996—at Chasen's restaurant in West Hollywood, California—Nancy Reagan raises her glass to a portrait of her husband in celebration of his 85th birthday.

On Reagan's 90th birthday, Nancy appeared on the *Larry King Show* to talk about her husband and their relationship. She spoke about Alzheimer's and the day that she and Reagan sat down to write the letter, letting Americans know that he had the disease. During the interview, Nancy said that the hardest part of all for her was no longer being able to share memories together. When asked if it wouldn't be better perhaps for Reagan to go to a center that specialized in working with Alzheimer's patients, however, Nancy's reaction was a definite "never." She would remain by Reagan's side to the very last—as she had since their wedding day and throughout their 50-plus-year marriage—loving and nurturing him.

Reagan's condition slowly deteriorated as the years went by. Although his health, other than the Alzheimer's, was excellent, this devastating disease had taken away the man that Nancy and the country had loved for so many years.

A fall in 2001 broke his right hip, and the following surgery involved pins, plates, and screws. The outpouring of good wishes for this past president was incredible. The Reagan Presidential Library received more than 10,000 e-mails, and Nancy received calls from former Presidents Ford and Bush, current President Bush, and Prince Charles. Although Reagan healed quickly from his fracture, it still put an end to his walks with Nancy. He could no longer ride or swim.

Nancy and Ronald Reagan

Nevertheless, on his birthday in 2002, at 91, Reagan became the longest living president. In that same year, he and Nancy were presented with the Congressional Gold Medal, the highest honor bestowed by the United States Congress. Reagan was honored for his work toward freedom and a better economy, while Nancy was honored for work to prevent drug abuse through the "Just Say No" campaign.

Initiated by the Ronald Reagan Legacy Project in Washington, D.C., a movement is underway to proclaim February 6th as Ronald Reagan Day. The organization, founded in 1997, would also like to see Reagan's face put on the ten-dollar bill and on license plates. Thanks to this group's efforts, in 2002, Dixon, Illinois, renamed a portion of Hennepin Avenue, the street Reagan had lived on as a child, "Reagan Way." The street includes his boyhood home, school, and church and ends at Lowell Park, where he worked so long as a lifeguard.

Ronald Reagan was, indeed, a man of charm and courage, a man of vision and determination. The Lowell Park lifeguard, the determined Gipper, and the suntanned California governor all remained inside him, guiding him to the greatness that he achieved. His father's belief in racial equality and his mother's lessons of strong faith served him well throughout his life. Reagan's actions led to the end of the Cold War, the fall of the Berlin Wall, and the reunification of Germany. His words and images helped America regain its pride and self-confidence. He made Americans believe once again in the unlimited potential of the nation in which they were living. Reagan's leadership reflected his deep love of the nation and its people.

Referring to his nickname, "The Great Communicator," in his farewell address from the Oval Office on January 11, 1989, Reagan put it this way: "I wasn't a great communicator, but I communicated great things, and they didn't spring full bloom from my brow, they came from the heart of a great nation—from our experience, our wisdom, and our belief in the principles that have guided us for two centuries. They called it the Reagan revolution. Well, I'll accept that, but for me it always seemed more the great rediscovery, a rediscovery of our values and our common sense."[3]

---

[3]Lou Cannon, *Ronald Reagan: The Presidential Portfolio*, 281.

Chapter Ten

A Hero Is Laid to Rest

As a nation mourns one of its most-beloved patriots, the courage and strength of Ronald Reagan carry on.

The last ten years of Ronald Reagan's life were in stark contrast to how he lived the first 83 years of his life. After several decades in the spotlight, first as an actor and then as a politician, he had faded from sight as the effects of Alzheimer's disease took control. The last photograph the public saw was from his 89th-birthday celebration—an intimate moment between Reagan and his wife, Nancy. After that, Nancy kept the nation up to date on how he was doing—and for a long time, he did amazingly well. While the disease stole away his memories, his body stayed strong and healthy. It was a tragedy to lose such a great man in such slow increments.

At a fund-raiser for Alzheimer's in May 2004, Nancy said that her husband had now gone to a place where she could no longer reach him. Less than a month later, on June 5, the end finally came. At the age of 93, Reagan lost the ten-year-long battle with Alzheimer's disease at his home in the Los Angeles neighborhood of Bel Air. Nancy, Patti, and Ron, Jr., were at his side when he passed away. According to an article written by Patti Davis in *People* magazine, the last moment was a poignant one. After many days in which his eyes remained closed, Reagan opened his eyes, and with complete clarity he looked at the woman who had been at his side for 52 years. It was a true testament to the endurance and power of a special love.

Nancy Reagan follows as military pallbearers bring the casket holding her husband to the Ronald Reagan Presidential Library in Simi Valley, California.

When the announcement of his death reached the public, the response was tremendous. Condolences poured in from around the world, and Americans sent thousands of sympathy cards and letters. President Bush ordered all flags lowered to half-mast for 30 days and declared June 11 to be a national day of mourning. The funeral arrangements began on Monday and lasted until Reagan's interment on Friday.

Behind the flag-draped coffin are Nancy Reagan, seated, their daughter, Patti, and their son, Ron, standing to her immediate left, and to the far right is Reagan's son, Michael.

For the first two days, the flag-covered casket was placed in the Ronald Reagan Presidential Library in Simi Valley. On Monday morning,

The caisson carrying President Reagan proceeds up Constitution Avenue en route to the U.S. Capitol. Reagan's riding boots are in the stirrups of the riderless horse, Sergeant York. The placement of backward boots is a 19th-century tradition of the U.S. Army cavalry.

Former first lady Nancy Reagan views the casket of her husband as she sits in the rotunda of the U.S. Capitol. Ronald Reagan is the tenth president to lie in state.

former Senator John Danforth of Missouri, an ordained Episcopal priest, presided over a private ceremony. Wearing a black suit and pearls, Nancy took a moment to caress the flag and gently lay her cheek on her husband's casket.

Public viewing began at noon Monday, and by the time it ended at 6 P.M. Tuesday, more than 100,000 people had walked by to pay homage to the former president. Families came from all over the country, even people who were too young to remember Reagan in office. California Governor Arnold Schwarzenegger and wife Maria Shriver stood in silent prayer by the casket.

Wednesday, a motorcade transported the president's casket to Ventura County Naval Base in Point Mugu, California. A military band playing "Hail to the Chief," as well as "Amazing Grace," and an artillery unit's 21-gun salute accompanied the transfer. There the coffin was put on an airplane and flown to Andrews Air Force Base outside Washington, D.C. At 6 P.M., the funeral procession to the Capitol began. It was the first state funeral held in Washington since President Lyndon Baines Johnson's in 1973.

A horse-drawn caisson pulled Reagan's coffin up Constitution Avenue to the Capitol. Alongside was a riderless horse to indicate a fallen leader, and in the stirrups were a pair of Reagan's boots. They were turned backward to signify the loss of a rider. At the western steps of the Capitol building, 21 planes flew over in tribute, and the last four were in the "missing man" formation. Once the casket reached the Capitol, it was placed on top of a catafalque that had been built in 1865 for Abraham Lincoln's coffin.

Public viewing began in Washington at 8:30 P.M. Wednesday night. Once again, people came from near and far to pay tribute to their former president. Many stood in line as long as seven hours, and the Red Cross handed out blankets to keep them warm through the night. Approximately 5,000 mourners walked through the Capitol Rotunda every hour. An estimated 105,000 in all paid their respects. All of these events were kept under intense levels of security, with protection being provided by a combination of the Secret Service, the FBI, the State Highway Patrol, and the local police.

The Reagan family was touched and surprised at the outpouring of emotion from people around the country. More than double the number of people came to view Reagan than had been anticipated. Many of them came to honor Nancy as well, holding signs and shouting that they loved and appreciated her years of caring for her "Ronnie." At almost 81, Nancy held together with grace and elegance, despite her frail frame. The relationship she shared with Reagan for more than half a century has earned her admiration and appreciation the world over.

Reagan is only the 30th American and the 10th president ever to lie in state, an honor that began in 1852, when Senator Henry Clay of Kentucky died. From humble beginnings, Ronald Reagan went on to become one of the most-beloved American heroes.

As light rain fell on the nation's capital, funeral services were held at the Washington National Cathedral for former President Ronald Reagan. Nancy Reagan is holding the arm of President George W. Bush while other former presidents and their wives look on.

Michael Reagan stands with Patti and Ron as they comfort their mother during the burial service at the Ronald Reagan Presidential Library. Nancy is holding the flag that once draped her husband's coffin.

A Chronology of Reagan's Life

February 6, 1911: Born in Tampico, Illinois.

1932: Graduates from Eureka College, Eureka, Illinois.

1932–1937: Works as radio announcer at WOC, Davenport, Iowa; and then WHO, Des Moines, Iowa.

1937: Makes his film debut with *Love Is on the Air.*

January 26, 1940: Marries Jane Wyman, actress. Children: Maureen, born 1941; Michael (adopted), born 1945; and Christine, born four months premature in 1947 and died the next day. Marriage ends in divorce in 1949.

1947: Becomes president of the Screen Actors Guild.

March 4, 1952: Marries Nancy Davis, actress. Children: Patti, born 1952; and Ronald, born 1958.

October 27, 1964: Gives celebrated speech in favor of GOP presidential candidate Barry Goldwater.

November 8, 1966: Elected California governor, defeating incumbent Edmund G. Brown.

November 3, 1970: Elected to second term as California governor.

November 4, 1980: Elected President of the United States over incumbent Jimmy Carter, garnering 51.6 percent of the popular vote to 41.7 percent for Carter and 6.7 percent for independent John Anderson.

January 20, 1981: Sworn in as 40th President of the United States.

March 30, 1981: Wounded by one of six shots fired as he left a Washington hotel after giving a speech.

September 1981: Fulfills pledge to nominate the first woman to the U.S. Supreme Court. Arizona judge Sandra Day O'Conner becomes a member of the high court.

November 6, 1984: Re-elected, defeating former Vice President Walter Mondale with nearly 60 percent of the popular vote.

November 19–21, 1985: Summit in Geneva with Soviet leader Mikhail Gorbachev. Reagan calls it a "fresh start" in U.S.–Soviet relations.

May 29–June 2, 1988: Summit in Moscow. Reagan and Gorbachev exchange ratified texts of the INF treaty, discuss strategic and conventional arms, and stroll in Red Square.

November 1990: Publishes his memoir, *An American Life.*

November 4, 1991: Ronald Reagan Presidential Library in Simi Valley, California, is dedicated, with President Bush and former Presidents Reagan, Carter, Ford, and Nixon in attendance.

November 5, 1994: Discloses he had been diagnosed with Alzheimer's disease.

March 4, 2001: Christening of the aircraft carrier *Ronald Reagan.*

August 8, 2001: Becomes the longest-lived president, having lived 33,120 days. President John Adams lived 33,119 days.

July 12, 2003: U.S. Navy commissions its newest aircraft carrier, the USS *Ronald Reagan,* the first carrier to be named for a living president.

June 5, 2004: Reagan dies at age 93.

Tributes to an American Icon

"I think they broke the mold when they made Ronnie."
—Nancy Reagan

"A truly great American hero. . . . He will be missed not only by those who knew him and not only by the nation that he served so proudly and loved so deeply, but also by millions of men and women who live in freedom today because of the policies he pursued."
—Former British Prime Minister Margaret Thatcher

"Reagan was a statesman who, despite all disagreements that existed between our countries at the time, displayed foresight and . . . arrange[d] normal relations between our countries."
—Former Soviet leader Mikhail Gorbachev

"Hillary and I will always remember President Ronald Reagan for the way he personified the indomitable optimism of the American people, and for keeping America at the forefront of the fight for freedom for people everywhere."
—Former President Bill Clinton

"President Ronald Reagan proved that an American, raised in difficult family circumstance, in a small town, with no personal money, could not only succeed but could rise to lead the cause of freedom. . . . His principled policies proved that . . . all people everywhere deserve the right to dream, to pursue their dreams, and to govern themselves."
—Former House Speaker Newt Gingrich

Among the flowers and flags placed outside the funeral home in Santa Monica, California, were these words from Matthew 25:21 in which the Lord commends the work of his servant and welcomes his servant into his presence.

"This is a sad hour in the life of America. A great American life has just come to an end. . . . Ronald Reagan won America's respect with his greatness and won its love with his goodness. He had the confidence that comes with conviction, the strength that comes with character, the grace that comes with humility and the humor that comes with wisdom. He leaves behind a nation he restored and a world he helped save. During the years of President Reagan, America laid to rest an era of division and self-doubt. And because of his leadership, the world laid to rest an era of fear and tyranny. Now, in laying our leader to rest, we say thank you. He always told us that for America the best was yet to come. We comfort ourselves in the knowledge that this is true for him, too. His work is done and now a shining city awaits him. May God bless Ronald Reagan."
—President George W. Bush

1911–2004